AZZEDINE ALAÏA

A COUTURIER'S COLLECTION

Ten years on from the major retrospective celebrating the work of couturier Azzedine Alaïa, the Palais Galliera now pays tribute to him in an exhibition drawn from his personal fashion collection.

Azzedine Alaïa was born in Tunisia and moved to Paris in 1956 to develop his technical skills and open a studio. He produced his first collection in the early 1980s and quickly made a name for himself, both in France and on the international stage, gaining even greater recognition in 1989, when he designed a dress in the colours of the French flag to be worn in the parade celebrating the bicentenary of the French Revolution.

As well as being a couturier, there was another side to Azzedine Alaïa, which this exhibition explores. He was also a collector who was passionate about fashion history, an expert with a keen eye who tracked down and preserved many pieces, some of which were one of a kind, such as Henri Matisse's stage costumes, which can be seen at the Paris Museum of Modern Art. The exhibition features clothes designed by some of the most iconic names in fashion alongside works by designers who have been largely forgotten. Through Alaïa's eyes, we can follow the evolution of the fashion world from the 19th century up until his death in 2017.

I am delighted that this exhibition, which takes visitors on an extraordinary journey through France's fashion heritage, is being held in Paris, the spiritual home of the fashion world. I would like to thank the Palais Galliera, which put together the exhibition in partnership with the Fondation Azzedine Alaïa. The Fondation's headquarters at 18 rue de la Verrerie, which were fully renovated by Azzedine Alaïa, testify to the couturier's love for the beauty of this city.

Presenting this collection to the public is a way of paying tribute both to one of the greatest couturiers in history and to fashion itself.

Anne Hidalgo
Mayor of Paris

no. 35
Madeleine Vionnet
'Little Horses'
evening gown
Haute couture,
autumn–winter 1921–22
Cream silk crepe with
beaded embroidery
by Lesage
FAA.VIO.0004

In 2013, the Palais Galliera reopened its doors with a retrospective celebrating the work of Azzedine Alaïa and his contribution to fashion history. Accompanied by Olivier Saillard, who was director of the museum at the time and curated the exhibition, Alaïa was visibly emotional when he spoke to the press: 'A retrospective is always a great honour, especially when it takes place during your lifetime!' With characteristic passion and dedication, the couturier decided not to produce a collection for that season so that he could instead pour all his efforts into the exhibition. The show was a success with critics and the public alike, and proved to be a major milestone in the history of the Palais Galliera.

At the launch of the exhibition, Azzedine Alaïa also spoke publicly about one of his most closely guarded secrets: his desire to create a foundation to showcase the impressive fashion collection that he had built up over the years. 'It's about preserving our heritage,' he explained, convinced that this was vital work. He revealed some of the iconic names that featured in his collection, from Balenciaga and Vionnet to Schiaparelli and Madame Grès, whose work he admired and wanted to preserve for future generations.

In this regard, Azzedine Alaïa was following in the footsteps of major figures in fashion history, such as Maurice Leloir, who founded the Société de l'Histoire du Costume and whose collection of historical clothing was donated to the City of Paris in 1920, and eventually became part of the Musée de la Mode's archive. Working closely with the Fondation Azzedine Alaïa, the Palais Galliera is now honoured to display the couturier's extraordinary collection and to pay tribute to him once again for his invaluable contribution to French fashion heritage.

I would like to thank Carla Sozzani, President of the Fondation Azzedine Alaïa, and Olivier Saillard, Director of the Fondation Azzedine Alaïa, for this valuable collaboration and for their tireless work preserving and promoting fashion heritage and securing Azzedine Alaïa's legacy.

Miren Arzalluz
Director of the Palais Galliera, Musée de la Mode de la Ville de Paris

no. 4
Cristóbal Balenciaga
'Mozart' costume worn by Barbara Hutton to Charles de Beistegui's masquerade ball, held on 14 September 1951 at the Palazzo Labia, Venice Jacket in the Louis XV style, silk velvet with embroidery by Rébé.
FAA.BAL.0032.1-2

For the last five years, the Fondation Azzedine Alaïa has been actively engaged in preserving the couturier's work and legacy. Alaïa arrived in Paris in 1956 and set up his legendary couture house, studios and home in the heart of the Marais district. The grand hall where he held his iconic runway shows now hosts exhibitions that continue Alaïa's mission of celebrating fashion heritage. An underground storage space ensures that his designs are preserved to the highest standards, just as they would be in a museum.

Azzedine Alaïa dreamed of becoming one of the great couturiers. His technical prowess and masterful cuts established his reputation among the most iconic names in fashion history, alongside figures such as Cristóbal Balenciaga and Madeleine Vionnet.

While the Tunisian-born designer sought to rival the greatest names in haute couture, he also cared deeply about preserving their work and their legacy. Starting in 1968, he proved to be an extraordinary collector, displaying relentless tenacity coupled with a clear vision. Driven by a fervent passion for fashion history, he built up an impressive collection of clothing from across different eras, featuring an almost inconceivable range of pieces. He amassed hundreds, even thousands of the most iconic dresses in fashion history, as well as the most prestigious brands. He never – or very rarely – exhibited them, choosing not to display these works that were at risk of being lost, but preserving this valuable heritage for the fashion world and for France.

Ten years after it honoured Azzedine Alaïa with his first retrospective in Paris, the Palais Galliera is now presenting a carefully honed selection of the treasures in his collection. This exhibition is an invitation to discover Alaïa the collector, the expert, the insatiable historian, the ever-inquisitive genius who did everything in his power to preserve the heritage of the fashion world.

In memory of the couturier and on behalf of the foundation that bears his name, on behalf of the board of directors, his friends and admirers, I would like to thank the City of Paris, the Palais Galliera and the Musée d'Art Moderne de Paris for making it possible to pay him such an affectionate and vital tribute.

Carla Sozzani
President of the Fondation Azzedine Alaïa

Azzedine Alaïa
arranging a Vionnet
dress on a mannequin,
1990. Photograph by
Patricia Canino.

CONTENTS

PRESERVING FASHION HERITAGE: FROM MAURICE LELOIR TO AZZEDINE ALAÏA

Miren Arzalluz

The sphere of fashion heritage in France has been shaped by the tastes and determination of a handful of collectors who, from the 19th century onwards, made it their mission to promote the historical and artistic importance of clothing. A succession of artists, art dealers, manufacturers and couturiers, all from outside the world of museums and universities, built up vibrant collections that they studied and analysed, as well as looking to them for reference and to find inspiration for their own work. From Maurice Leloir to Azzedine Alaïa, these knowledgeable amateurs were the first curators in the emerging discipline of fashion heritage and their work was instrumental in forming the fashion museums that would later come into being.[1]

The painter and illustrator Maurice Leloir played a crucial role in preserving fashion heritage and promoting the study of the discipline more broadly. Born into a family of artists, Leloir was the son of Héloïse Colin and the nephew of Anaïs Toudouze, two of the most prolific fashion illustrators of the 19th century. At a time when history painting and genre painting were enjoying growing popularity, he built up a large collection of objects, fabrics and historical costumes in his studio, which he used to faithfully recreate genre scenes from the 17th and 18th centuries in exquisite detail (figs. 1 and 5).

Leloir soon became known as an expert on historical clothing in France and had a major influence on early fashion exhibitions. The mid-19th century saw a number of national exhibitions designed to showcase the products of French industry, precursors to the Universal Exhibitions that were held in Paris from 1855 onwards. At the Universal Exhibition of 1900, a commission led by the painter Georges Cain, who had been head curator at the Musée Carnavalet in Paris since 1897, presented what was called the Musée Rétrospectif. This included a large section dedicated to fashion accessories as well as a selection of historical costumes, mainly from the 18th century. In his foreword to the exhibition catalogue, Cain wrote: 'The painter Maurice Leloir, a man of great generosity as well as great talent, offered us his unparalleled collection of women's clothing from the Louis XV and Louis XVI eras.'[2] A photograph published in the catalogue shows Leloir wearing a yellow silk brocade dressing gown that dates to 1840[3] (fig. 2) – this piece from his own collection was featured in the exhibition.

In 1906, Leloir founded the Société de l'Histoire du Costume (SHC) with the artists and collectors Édouard Detaille and François Carnot. Its first meeting was held on 10 January 1907 and its main aims were to create a fashion museum

2

Previous pages:
Fig. 1
Early 18th-century
costume, photograph
attributed to Maurice
Leloir, c. 1885.
Palais Galliera, Musée de la
Mode de la Ville de Paris

These pages:
Fig. 2
Portrait of Maurice Leloir
wearing a yellow silk
dressing gown, 1840

Fig. 3
Maurice Leloir (?) setting
up the 'Historical Costume'
exhibition held by the
Société de l'Histoire du
Costume in the great hall
of the Musée des Arts
Décoratifs, 6 May–
10 October 1909.
Photograph by Rol
Photo Agency

in Paris and to promote 'greater knowledge about clothing styles […], the preservation and restoration of historical clothing [and] the annual collection of modern fashion samples for future generations'.[4] In order to make public institutions more aware of fashion heritage, in May 1909 the SHC decided to hold its first major exhibition, called 'Historical Costume', in the Marsan Pavilion at the Musée des Arts Décoratifs (fig. 3). Realistic mannequins wearing historical garments and replicas were exhibited in large display cases, alongside a wide variety of accessories, furniture, fabrics and upholstery. Encouraged by the success of the exhibition, Leloir and his partners decided to open a costume museum based in the former studio of the artist Raimundo de Madrazo. This museum, tracing the evolution of fashion in France from the 16th to the 19th century, was opened by the President of France, Raymond Poincaré, on 23 January 1920 (fig. 4). In December of the same year, the SHC donated its entire collection of historical costumes to the City of Paris, with the aim of creating a permanent museum dedicated to fashion and its history. This donation formed the founding collection of what would become the Musée de la Mode de la Ville de Paris, based in the Palais Galliera since 1977.

Leloir's partners and the members of the SHC included some very influential figures in the worlds of contemporary fashion and culture: Gaston and Jean-Philippe Worth, the sons and heirs of Charles Frederick Worth, and Jacques Doucet. Alongside their work as fashion designers and directors of iconic couture houses, these famous couturiers also showed a profound understanding and sincere interest in fashion history and cared deeply about preserving its heritage.

After opening his couture house in 1858, Charles Frederick Worth built up a solid reputation as an official couturier to the major European royal families, and his work was highly sought after by aristocrats, actresses and women who belonged to the new, dynamic industrial middle classes on both sides of the Atlantic. He incorporated elements of 16th-, 17th- and 18th-century dress into his designs to create a distinctive historical style that marked his ballgowns and his stage costumes. Worth drew inspiration from the museums and galleries of Paris and London, but also from his own large collection of costumes, fabrics and historical etchings, which his sons inherited and continued to expand. In an interview after the death of his father in 1896, Jean-Philippe Worth said: 'As to where I get my ideas: sometimes from a piece of old Church embroidery or a scrap of Louis Quinze brocade, picked up in an old curiosity

3

shop. Often I have reconstituted a whole piece of material from a small breadth taken out of a Court costume or vestment. When I am satisfied […] with a design, it is reproduced to my order in different schemes of colouring, and even of material.'[5]

The Worth collection was therefore a living collection, amassed with great care as part of a dynamic creative process. The list of pieces that the Worth family loaned to the 'Historical Costume' exhibition, published in the catalogue, testifies to the scale and range of the collection: a 'little red velvet coat dyed with madder and embellished with silver embroidery, 17th century', a 'child's dress made of red velvet with gold embroidery, 18th century', a 'Louis XVI waistcoat made of pink silk covered in lace' and a 'white silk coat embroidered with multicoloured flowers' were among the pieces from the Worth collection that were on show for the Parisian public to admire. In an article about the process of planning and creating this first exhibition by the SHC, Leloir included a long section dedicated to one of the oldest pieces from the Worth collection: a 'Spanish corset which we placed on a mannequin in the central display case in the first room. […] I found this corset in the two Mr Worths' collection of embroidered fabrics, which they very kindly laid out for me

to look through, inviting me to choose whatever I thought was worthy of featuring in our exhibition'.[6] Gaston and Jean-Philippe Worth's involvement in this exhibition demonstrates their commitment to showcasing historical costume and promoting fashion heritage in France.

Another renowned designer who worked with Maurice Leloir was the collector and patron Jacques Doucet. He was one of the founders of the SHC in 1906 and its first treasurer (fig. 6). At the time, Doucet had amassed a large collection of 18th-century art, including paintings, sculptures, drawings and etchings, pieces of furniture and objets d'art. In 1912, he took the radical decision to sell his entire collection, in a series of extravagant auctions that sent shockwaves through the art market both within France and internationally. Doucet embarked on a new phase of life, as a collector of works by modern masters such as Degas, Cézanne, Manet and Van Gogh and a patron of contemporary artists such as Matisse, Picasso, Braque, Modigliani and Picabia. Alongside this work, he founded the Bibliothèque d'Art et d'Archéologie, now the library of the Institut National d'Histoire de l'Art (INHA), as well as the Bibliothèque Littéraire Jacques Doucet.

Recognized as one of the greatest collectors of his time, today Doucet is still a subject of

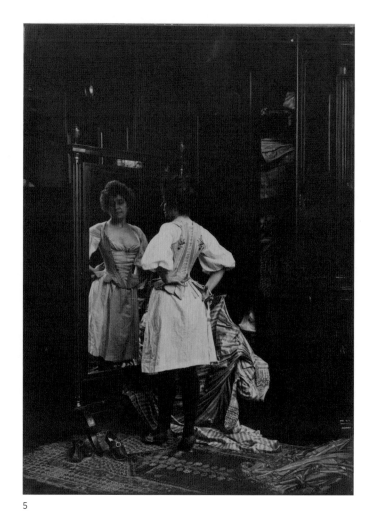

admiration and considerable academic interest. There have been a number of studies of his work, and a recent research project led by the INHA aims to build up a database of items that featured in his collections before they were sold off, in order to understand how unique they were and what an important role they played in the history of art. Countless works have been identified, but none of them are textiles or historical costumes. However, Doucet's involvement with the SHC, as well as numerous references to items donated to the project, show that he was interested in studying, preserving and exhibiting historical fashions. To cite one example, in 1910, the *Bulletin de la Société de l'Histoire du Costume* informed its members of a recent donation of a 'white satin dress, dating to 1735 or 1740. Donated by Mr Jacques Doucet. This dress, which still has its full lining of yellow taffeta with green, white and red stripes, has not undergone any modification and has preserved all the purity of its form.'[7] The information was accompanied by a photograph showing a young woman wearing the dress in question. This sack-back gown, along with an 18th-century gentleman's ensemble, are now part of the Palais Galliera collection.

After the SHC donated its collection, it was stored at the Musée Carnavalet. From 1943 onwards, it was under the care of Madeleine

Delpierre, who undertook the work of studying the collection, drawing up an inventory and exhibiting it. In 1954, working under Jacques Wilhelm, head curator at the Musée Carnavalet, she helped to stage the exhibition 'Dress in France in the 18th Century (1715–1789)'.[8] The success of the exhibition was an important factor leading to the creation of the Musée de la Mode de la Ville de Paris in 1956. Housed in rooms on the ground floor of the Musée d'Art Moderne de Paris, the new museum, considered an annexe of the Musée Carnavalet, opened its doors on 23 November 1956 with the exhibition 'Dress in France from the 16th to the 20th Century'.[9] From 1957 to 1971, Madeleine Delpierre continued to hold exhibitions that examined the history of fashion through different lenses: eras, types of clothing, techniques, and major donations or donors. In 1977, the City of Paris decided to move the newly named Musée de la Mode et du Costume de la Ville de Paris permanently to the Palais Galliera. The first exhibition held there was 'Paris 1945–1975: Elegance and Creativity',[10] which traced the recent history of haute couture.

After the museum's inauguration, Madeleine Delpierre received another extraordinary donation: the couturier Cristóbal Balenciaga's personal collection of historical clothing and textiles (figs. 7–10). In March 1979, seven years

Fig. 6
Jacques Doucet, 1920,
photographer unknown.
Library of the Institut
National d'Histoire de l'Art
(INHA), Paris, Jacques
Doucet collection

7

8

9

10

after his death, his family gave the Palais Galliera 'a range of pieces collected by the couturier as resources for his personal use', including 92 historical pieces: garments from the 18th and 19th centuries, ballgowns and stage costumes from the same period, Spanish and European traditional dress, clerical garments and fabrics. Balenciaga had built up his collection in an intuitive and spontaneous way, over the course of frequent visits to second-hand shops and flea markets in Paris and Madrid. Today, this collection reflects his aesthetic tastes and the diverse references that he drew on to create his designs. In a similar way to Worth, Balenciaga incorporated the broad range of pieces that he had acquired into his creative process; 19th-century silhouettes, embroidery from clerical garments, elements of traditional costume, lace and jet all appeared in the Basque couturier's collections, from when he arrived in Paris in 1937 until he closed his couture house in 1968.

In June 1970, Balenciaga had already made a major donation: eight prototype designs from his collections between 1951 and 1968.[11]

When he closed the couture house in May 1968, he had decided to keep a selection of pieces that he considered significant and that embodied the best of his work, so that they could be put on public display in the collections of the Musée de la Mode.

Despite this decision, and because his retirement was so sudden, a number of prototypes that had been stored at the Balenciaga headquarters over the years, along with fabric offcuts, accessories and all kinds of supplies that were still in the studios, were sold off or scattered. Azzedine Alaïa, then a young, talented couturier who was already well known for his technical prowess, was invited by Mademoiselle Renée, a close collaborator of Balenciaga's and his studio director, to take whatever he thought would be interesting and useful for his own work. Alaïa was moved by the tragic end of this illustrious fashion house that he admired so deeply, and he was inspired to take a number of the master couturier's works to ensure they would not be forgotten. It was the first step in amassing one of the largest fashion collections in the world.

1
Maude Bass-Krueger, 'Fashion Collections, Collectors, and Exhibitions in France, 1874–1900: Historical Imagination, the Spectacular Past, and the Practice of Restoration', *Fashion Theory*, vol. 22, no. 4–5, 2018, pp. 405–433.

2
Georges Cain, 'Préface', in *Musée rétrospectif des classes 85 & 86. Le costume et ses accessoires à l'Exposition universelle internationale de 1900 à Paris*, Saint-Cloud: Belin Frères, 1900, p. 12.

3
Ibid, p. 58

4
Society of the History of Costume, *Statutes*, Article 1, Paris: E. Letombe, 1907, p. 3.

5
Marie A. Belloc, 'La Maison Worth: An Interview with Mr Jean Worth', *The Lady's Realm*, London, vol. 1, 1896–97, p. 142.

6
Maurice Leloir, 'À propos de la première exposition de costumes anciens', *Bulletin de la Société de l'histoire du costume*, no. 7–8, April–July 1909, pp. 158–163 and 165.

7
Bulletin de la Société de l'histoire du costume, no. 9, January 1910, p. 6.

8
9 November 1954–59 January 1995.

9
1 November 1956–1 February 1957.

10
May–August 1977.

11
GAL1970.92.1 to 8.

AZZEDINE ALAÏA: A PASSION FOR FRENCH COUTURE

Olivier Saillard

'Fashion is an invention, elegance is truth.'
– Azzedine Alaïa

One of the great couturiers of the 20th century, Azzedine Alaïa was renowned for his knowledge and mastery of the techniques of cutting and assembling a garment. His unfailingly high standards meant that he could spend many years refining a jacket or a coat, until the sewing stage imposed its own rigour and definitive form. In the distinctive collections that he created between 1979 and 2017, Alaïa invented a new silhouette, with its own unique form of architecture, which to this day refuses to conform to fashions and trends. At first glance, his designs may appear understated, but their technical ingenuity and timeless elegance shine through.

Alongside his work as a designer, Alaïa was also ahead of his time as a collector of clothing and documentation that traced the history of fashion. From 1968 onwards, he became a trailblazer, buying and preserving examples of fashion heritage, whether haute couture, ready-to-wear or everyday garments.

Over the course of many decades, before fashion houses started to recognize the importance of preserving their own heritage and set up dedicated archives worthy of major museums, Azzedine Alaïa was quietly amassing extensive collections of clothes that represented different eras of fashion history, from its earliest days in the late 19th century up to the present day.

Unable to stand by and watch his own craft's cultural heritage be scattered, Alaïa collected first hundreds, then thousands of pieces by the designers that he most admired. He built up his collection until it was all-encompassing, bringing together the works of couturiers whose names had often faded into obscurity but were now resurrected and restored to their rightful place in fashion history.

This all-consuming passion drove him to acquire beautiful pieces by Madeleine Vionnet, Paul Poiret, Jean Patou, Cristóbal Balenciaga and Madame Grès, all labels that feature prominently in his collection. Items from the earliest days of haute couture in the 19th century, including some designed by Charles Frederick Worth and Redfern, also appear in the inventory. Always on the lookout for a masterpiece and stopping at nothing to acquire it, Alaïa also liked to choose pieces that testified to the work of the entire studio, as he always championed the importance and inventiveness of this skilled craft work. For this reason, some truly striking pieces by Elsa Schiaparelli, among others, and stage costumes designed by the artist Henri Matisse[1] sit alongside clothes intended to be worn in everyday life.

1

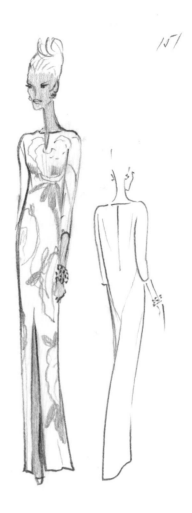

2

Over the course of more than fifty years, without ever exhibiting it publicly, Alaïa built up the largest private fashion collection in the world, which also included countless accessories, photographs, drawings and signed sketches. Cared for by the foundation set up in his name, where the process of drawing up a full inventory, restoring pieces and storing them carefully is still ongoing, this collection is made up of many thousands of designs.

Because of his work preserving this incredible cultural heritage for France and for the fashion world, Azzedine Alaïa is more than a revolutionary couturier who moved from Tunis to Paris and made a name for himself on the global stage. He is also recognized as a true archivist, a passionate historian, following in the footsteps of Maurice Leloir, whose collection was instrumental in the founding of the Palais Galliera. A selection of almost 140 pieces that best represent his taste for timeless design are presented here for the first time.

Azzedine Alaïa set himself apart from his contemporaries, and from those designers who came before him, as he was the only one to amass a fashion and costume collection so vast that today it rivals those of many of the greatest museums in the world. Unlike other designers who basked in the light of the empires they had

built, Alaïa was a secret historian who ensured that all their legacies would be remembered. Attending auctions and private sales, he often outbid museum directors and curators. He was obsessed with the illustrious names and brands of the past that made up his personal fashion pantheon, and felt driven to possess and collect their work.

For Alaïa, these included Madeleine Vionnet, Cristóbal Balenciaga and Madame Grès. Their work was architectural or sculptural in nature and he recognized himself in them, as he shared their passion for technique and clever cutting. There are many hundreds of designs in his collection, both daywear and eveningwear, and some items are very rare and unusual.

It all began in 1968, when **Cristóbal Balenciaga** announced he was closing his couture studio in Paris. The iconic Spanish couturier had reigned supreme over the fashion world since he arrived in the French capital in 1937, but he could not find a place for himself among the new generation that was moving towards ready-to-wear fashions. Mademoiselle Renée, who was Balenciaga's studio director, knew Azzedine Alaïa, as he had established a reputation for himself since moving to Paris in 1956. He designed clothes commissioned by individual clients, appealing to a very select clientele, and was known for his technical prowess, so he was sometimes called on by other designers to finish off or construct more complex pieces. Mademoiselle Renée invited him to come to the studio and take any fabrics or dresses that might be useful to him in his own work.

Alaïa often spoke about how astounded he was by seeing Balenciaga's designs, true works of abstraction and weightlessness. Throughout his lifetime, up until a few months before his death, again and again Alaïa described the powerful and formative impression that these designs had made on him. When he heard that these garments, suits and evening gowns risked being lost when the Spanish couturier's fashion house closed, Alaïa was struck, probably for the first time, by the importance of preserving this slice of fashion heritage. In the late 1960s, there were only a handful of museums around the world that recognized the importance of fashion. Couture houses themselves treated their archives as unsold stock. Aware of how easily this legacy could be lost, as he'd seen when Balenciaga had closed, Alaïa took it upon himself to become the guardian of the looks and legacies that other designers had created. From then on, he started to acquire countless treasures from the fashion world, along with all the documentation that told the story of the studios and shed light on their creative work.

Alaïa probably wanted to see how his work measured up to the masterpieces created by designers who, like him, were driven by the quest for perfection of technique and cut that were almost undetectable in the final piece. It seems likely, but we can never be sure, because his collection quickly grew to such a size that he must have been driven by a kind of madness, as only an obsessive collector could have justified the sheer number of pieces that he was buying.

Azzedine Alaïa's attention quickly turned to the work of **Madeleine Vionnet**. Fascinated by her technical skill, he hunted down as many Vionnet designs as he could find on the market.

In the early 1980s, a well-known article published in *Jardin des modes* linked Alaïa's name to a famous dress designed by Madeleine Vionnet.[2] Cut on the bias and wound around the shoulders, this crepe dress had been immortalized in a series of photographs by George Hoyningen-Huene that were published in *Vogue*. The dress was in the collection of the Union Française des Arts du Costume (UFAC), whose director was Yvonne Deslandres, but its complex construction meant that its true form was swathed in mystery.[3] Alaïa was the only person who dared to take on the challenge of draping the dress on a wooden mannequin to show it to its full advantage. Working from a photograph of the piece taken in a three-way mirror, Alaïa succeeded in this task with flying colours. He repeated the feat a few years later for the photographer Patricia Canino, for a monograph being published on Madeleine Vionnet's work.[4] By closely studying the seams and decoding the fastenings and ties, the expert couturier solved the mystery of the dress's many sections and it took shape once again as the true masterpiece it was.

Alaïa played a major role in the resurgence of popularity that Madeleine Vionnet's work enjoyed. Aside from a few students and fashion historians, she had largely been forgotten for many decades. Alaïa was instrumental in staging the first international exhibition dedicated to Vionnet's work from the 1920s and 1930s,[5] which was held in 1991 at the Centre de la Vieille-Charité in Marseille. Vionnet's handkerchief dresses were displayed once again, showcasing the purity of cut for which the designer was famous.

Around the same time, Maryline Vigouroux invited Alaïa to become honorary president of the Institut Mode Méditerranée, an innovative project that included an association set up to promote the work of young designers in the Mediterranean region, a world-leading resource library, a museum and a growing archive collection, for which Alaïa acted as an advisor.

Madeleine Vionnet's designs began achieving record valuations at auctions, with many established and emerging fashion museums competing to buy pieces by the label.

Alaïa built up friendships with a number of dealers and experts, based around their shared interest in fashion heritage, and he drew on this network in his quest to acquire Vionnet designs for his own collection, as he admired her work perhaps just as much as Balenciaga's. Each of the day dresses and evening gowns that he acquired bear witness to the technical prowess that underpinned her work. Made of chiffon or spider tulle, devoré velvet or finely embroidered crepe, these garments display the designer's almost unparalleled knowledge and skill. Among the masterpieces in Alaïa's collection, there is one that is particularly exceptional: an ivory dress from the autumn–winter 1921 collection, embroidered by Lesage with a pattern of horses in a frieze design (no. 35, p. 23). Two similar designs are in the collections of the Musée des Arts Décoratifs in Paris and the Costume Institute at the Metropolitan Museum in New York.

Madame Grès was a contemporary of Madeleine Vionnet's in the 1930s and her draped creations share a certain ethereality. However, she

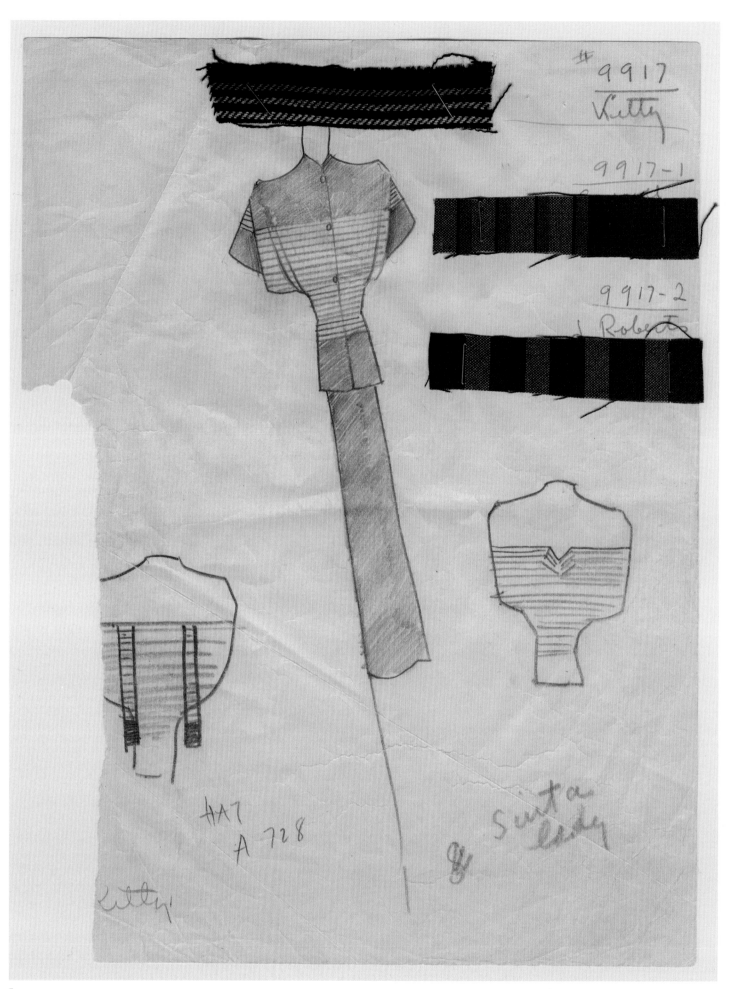

continued designing well into the late 1970s and early 1980s, enjoying an unusually long career for the fashion world, and she was a lone figure who refused to bow to trends.

Azzedine Alaïa had great admiration for Madame Grès. Whether designing for the label Alix or Grès,[6] she always managed to promote her own ideas of style, never yielding to the whims of fashion. When the first retrospective of her work was held at the Musée Bourdelle in 2011,[7] he agreed to lend three of his pieces. One of these, made of dark black fabric that draped around the bust and waist, showed that only a master couturier such as Grès, with a sculptor's touch, was able to rise to the challenge of creating a dress with the feel of a bas-relief.

The exhibition's curators and the museum directors had little idea how many designs by Madame Grès were in Alaïa's collection. It is unlikely that even Alaïa himself knew the true number, as Grès's designs were stored across many different locations in his archives. Now collected together in a storage facility that is specially adapted to preserve textiles, there are some 700 from across the many decades of her career. Long, exquisitely draped black jersey dresses from the time when Madame Grès was designing for the label Alix sit alongside draped pieces from the 1970s, with motifs inspired by Matisse. These are interspersed with a plethora of daywear and eveningwear designs that testify to the couturier's impressive skill as a sculptor of fabric. There is also a priceless collection of many hundreds of photographs of her work, taken by Robert Doisneau, Roger Schall and Eugène Rubin, among others, which together make up one of the largest collections of archive material in the fashion world.

The highlight of the collection, and one of the most unusual pieces Alaïa acquired, was a stage costume designed by Grès.[8] These fantastical garments, inspired by Hindu deities, were created for the dancer Muni, who had been a close friend and muse of Madame Grès's since 1937, and they now form part of the foundation's collection.

Alaïa's collection was built up over time around the work of these iconic couturiers – Balenciaga, Vionnet and Grès – as the designer saw himself as the sole heir to their legacies, continuing their techniques and practices. The collection was also shaped by visits to museums, exhibitions and collections, and the revelatory moments when Alaïa encountered a new designer's work for the first time.

It was on his first trip to New York in 1980 that Azzedine Alaïa discovered the works of American couturiers such as Charles James, Adrian and Claire McCardell. Their groundbreaking designs were inspired by haute couture but closer to high-end ready-to-wear. These designers were ushering in a new modern era, but French museums did not show much interest in their work and it hardly featured in their collections. However, the clothes created by these designers across the Atlantic soon grabbed Alaïa's attention.

In 1980, two years after the death of **Charles James**, a retrospective of his work was held at the Brooklyn Museum in New York. The luxury New York department store Bergdorf Goodman invited Azzedine Alaïa to stage a runway show in the city. The collection that he presented flung him into the spotlight, heralding him as one of the most influential designers of the decade. His use of perforated, studded leather and draped designs announced a new silhouette that would come to be a hallmark of his style. During his stay, Alaïa visited the Charles James exhibition. He hadn't known much about the designer's work and was impressed by his pattern-making skill, with some patterns that were as complex as maps of futuristic cities, testifying to his dedication to studying and achieving the perfect cut. The pieces on show, especially the full-skirted evening gowns, built up a picture of this designer, whom Alaïa saw as a kindred spirit.

The two designers were separated by many decades but shared the same philosophy. Both sought to keep their output low, unafraid to reject the rules that governed the fashion world. They both adopted a structuralist approach that relied more on a certain grammar than a style. James was content with creating only two hundred pieces that could be worn together in different combinations. Alaïa claimed that a single idea was enough to determine the fate of a new collection – it was up to the couturier to grab hold of it and guide it towards maturity. Many of the two designers' statements about their work have a similar feel and their clothes, while created around forty years apart, share the same spirit. The architectural nature of their designs enhanced the female body, using ingenious, liberating cuts. Charles James deliberately limited the number of pieces that he designed, which means that there are very few of his pieces to be found on the market. The only museum in France that has a few of his designs is the Musée des Arts Décoratifs, which includes one of his evening gowns in its collection. From the 1980s onwards, Azzedine Alaïa was keen to acquire pieces by James, as he inevitably saw much of himself reflected in the designer's work. One of the most beautiful Charles James pieces that he owned was a magnificent red evening gown (no. 10, p. 73).

Alaïa not only collected James's dresses and coats, but also drew on his principles. Like James, he was not afraid to say no, a trait that often got him into difficulties while it was instrumental in James's success.

Two other American designers add a touch of originality to Azzedine Alaïa's collection, setting it apart from those held by French museums. **Adrian**, a costume designer and couturier who was active from the 1930s to the 1950s, was behind some of Greta Garbo's most beautiful film costumes as well as haute couture collections created in his Beverly Hills studio, but his work is conspicuously absent from collections held by institutions in France. In the early 1980s, Azzedine Alaïa acquired almost 350 of Adrian's suits, day dresses and coats, evening gowns and formal dresses. It is thought that the couturier met Adrian's son and heir in person to finalize the contract for this sale, which was remarkable for the sheer number of pieces it included. The structured suits, single-breasted coats and sheath dresses – most of which were monochrome rather than printed – all testify to Alaïa's own love of timeless styles.

Alaïa's collection of Adrian pieces also includes an unusual level of documentation, with programmes from runway shows and original sketches from Adrian's personal archives (fig. 3) offering greater insight into his work as a designer in the U.S.

Azzedine Alaïa had a profound admiration for **Claire McCardell**'s pioneering and visionary ready-to-wear fashions from the 1930s, 1940s and 1950s. While her uncompromising designs were recognized as setting the tone for the new modern style, McCardell's avant-garde creations were not well represented in French collections. However, the collections held by the Fashion Institute of Technology and the Costume Institute in New York offer a wealth of material that allows her work to be appraised. Her designs often featured mesh fabric and she turned away from under-structures and padding, instead emphasizing comfort and unrestricted movement, achieving a practical elegance that is now acknowledged as undeniably innovative. The designs in Alaïa's collection – wrap dresses, coat dresses and swimwear – suggest that he was drawn to their timeless charm and ingenious cuts. Nowadays, the number of McCardell's designs on public display in France is sufficient for the public to build up a representative idea of her ambitious work, which has lost none of its modernity or its power to surprise.

Looking at the work of these master couturiers, we can discern Alaïa's taste for uncompromising design, where technical skill is more important than any embellishment. There are not many printed fabrics, aside from a few of McCardell and Adrian's pieces, which were influenced by contemporary artistic movements. Every shade of black, every swathe of red or intense blue used by these designers writes its own line in the story of fashion's evolution as told by Alaïa.

When it came to **Gabrielle Chanel**'s work, Azzedine Alaïa especially admired the designs from the early part of her career, such as the little black dress from 1927 and the long Romany-style dresses of the 1930s, when she was more interested in establishing her own style than following trends. When he was President of the Institut International de la Mode in Marseille, working closely with Maryline Vigouroux, Alaïa used his influence to convince the patrons to acquire their first Chanel collection. The resulting exhibition was a forerunner to what would later become the Musée de la Mode in Marseille.

Alaïa admired designers who were hands-on, who, like him, knew how to bend any fabric to their will and create a dress from it. But he was also fascinated by those who were his polar opposites, and he recognized in Chanel an ingenious stylist who succeeded in changing the course of fashion history not once, but twice. Her little black dress set out her manifesto, a declaration of intent that has still never been matched. The suits that she designed after reopening her couture house in 1954 looked to the future, while the uniform of tweed skirts and jackets made other designers look as if they were stuck in the past. Alaïa could not remain unmoved by that. He claimed to have sometimes worked for almost ten years on perfecting the same jacket, from one runway show to the next, so he was bound to be impressed by the consistency of Chanel's style. As well as the many Chanel suits and coats from the 1950s and the 1960s that feature in the Fondation Azzedine Alaïa's collection, there is also a carefully chosen selection of dresses from the 1930s, which illustrate what Alaïa admired most about her work – classic Parisian elegance combined with an uncompromising clarity of vision that ensured her designs stood the test of time.

In the early 1950s, Azzedine Alaïa was getting ready to leave his native Tunisia and move to Paris to pursue his dream of being a couturier. Before he left, he was entrusted with a letter and given instructions that it should be delivered directly to **Elsa Schiaparelli**. However, when the young man arrived at the Italian designer's studio, he was so intimidated that he ran away as soon as he had rung the bell, abandoning his mission. Later, when he finally met Schiaparelli,

Fig. 4
Telegram from
Elsa Schiaparelli,
Fondation Azzedine
Alaïa Collection, Paris

4

Alaïa told her about this letter, which she had never received because of him. She could not hide her distress when he told her who it was from. It seems that this person, who shall remain nameless, wanted to declare his love for her. Alaïa was plagued by guilt, but Schiaparelli herself reassured him. No one could remember whether the letter had been left on the front step, been forgotten on the doormat or blown away. Time did its work, and soon the young Alaïa's blunder was forgiven. Some years later, when Alaïa met the actress Arletty, he crossed paths with Schiaparelli again, and it soon became clear from their innovative use of zips that they all spoke the same language of design.[9]

To Schiaparelli, everything had a symbolic meaning, like a talisman or omen. The ceramic buttons on her suit jackets and her astrological embroidery motifs were like protective amulets for the women who wore them.

Alaïa did everything in his power to acquire dresses by this designer whose path had crossed with his a few years earlier and whose surrealist creations he knew well. One of his most beautiful acquisitions, the 'Zodiac' jacket from the autumn–winter 1938–39 collection (no. 46, p. 97), made of midnight blue velvet embellished with gold and silver stars, was bought for a record price. Alaïa carried his prize away proudly, like a totem

or a good luck charm. This jacket joined other iconic designs that were already in his collection, such as an evening gown embellished all over with rhodoid acetate sequins (no. 44, p. 98) and a dress with a print based on sketches by Marcel Vertès, from the spring–summer 1939 collection (no. 43, p. 101). Soon Alaïa would also acquire a number of embroidered jackets, embellished with unusual buttons.

Accessories, hats and tiny bags typical of the 1930s and 1950s were also added to the collection, which was rounded out by a series of rare written documents, including the complete correspondence maintained between Elsa Schiaparelli and her secretary during the war years (fig. 4). Alaïa also acquired a batch of dressmaker's toiles made for customers by the designer's atelier. Perhaps in an attempt to make up for the letter that he had lost, he was keen to preserve everything he could find that was connected with Schiaparelli, from a typed programme for a runway show to a sketch of a famous dress. In 2009, he staged an exhibition of Schiaparelli pieces that were about to be sold. Under the glass roof, in the grand hall where he held his runway shows, the public had the chance to admire Schiaparelli's famous jacket with embroidery based on a drawing by Jean Cocteau, among other masterpieces.[10]

5

A similar sale, four years earlier (figs. 5 and 6), had revealed Azzedine Alaïa's great love and admiration for the work of **Paul Poiret**.[11] The clothes came mainly from the personal wardrobe of Denise Poiret, the designer's wife, and included hundreds of exceptional pieces, all showcased in Alaïa's premises at 18 rue de la Verrerie in Paris (4th *arrondissement*). Some of the items remained there and now belong to the Fondation, including 'Moscovite', an asymmetric jacket worn by Denise Poiret in 1913 (no. 53, p. 107).

Alaïa understood Poiret's taste for the exotic. The couturier was ahead of his time, one of the first designers to draw on elements of folklore and historical clothing in his creative process. His collaboration with Raoul Dufy, whose original motifs appear on the lining of some pieces (no. 55, pp. 102–103), added a touch of unassuming elegance. Alaïa was deeply moved by the designer's sad tale, as Poiret went from being a celebrated couturier to ending his days in poverty, but that was not the only reason why he was interested in his work. Poiret was a true pioneer. He revolutionized the role of the couturier, so that they were no longer simply official suppliers for a specific set of clients but were setting the agenda themselves. Poiret rewrote the rulebook, incorporating the perfume industry into the world of fashion and pursuing his interest in the decorative arts. The designer's work features prominently in Alaïa's collections, including pieces from the 1910s, which drew inspiration from historical costumes in the Empire style, designs from the 1920s, which embraced a certain fashionable exoticism, and a number of children's garments. Again, the influence of folklore and traditional dress comes through strongly. The selection of clothes that belonged to Denise Poiret allows us to build up a picture of the styles worn by a woman of her time who was at the centre of the fashion world.

By examining the work of these designers, their principles and the records from their studios, Alaïa was able to trace their role in empowering women to take back control of their own appearance.

Alaïa was keen to ensure that his collection was complete and covered all eras, so he added garments and fashions from the 19th century. He was interested in the work of **Charles Frederick Worth**, the father of haute couture who moved from his native Britain to Paris, and he bought a number of his designs. A few *visites*,[12] coats, and dresses typical of popular styles capture the spirit of fashion at the turn of the century (nos. 66 to 68). Drawn to the luxurious fabrics – or sometimes,

Fig. 5
Exhibition view of
'Paul Poiret: La création
en liberté', Fondation
Azzedine Alaïa, Paris,
21–24 April 2005.
Fondation Azzedine
Alaïa Collection, Paris

Fig. 6
*Paul Poiret: La création
en liberté*, catalogue, Paris:
Paisa, 2005, 2 vols.
Fondation Azzedine
Alaïa Collection, Paris

6

by contrast, the use of simple, modest fabrics –
and unusual shapes, Alaïa added these pieces
to his growing collection.

The collection also features a number of
works by contemporaries of Worth's, such as
Redfern. With branches in both London and Paris,
Redfern was known for creating high-quality
suits and chic clothing for outdoor activities.
Alaïa must have admired the masterful cuts and
quality fabrics, a combination that marked these
designs out as ahead of their time (no. 69, p. 57).
Although older couture labels were harder to
find on the market, Alaïa made a concerted effort
to bolster his collection with designs from the
19th century. He concentrated on finding suits,
jackets and coats, the kind of garments that had
made his own name. Meanwhile, a day ensemble,
comprising a jacket and skirt embellished with
hydrangeas (no. 65, p. 61), celebrates the talents
of **Jacques Doucet**, a couturier active during the
late 19th and early 20th century, who was a lover
of literature and the arts.

Azzedine Alaïa took an avid interest in the
stylistic and artistic experiments of the early
20th century, particularly those of **Mariano
Fortuny**, who created his own unique approach
to design, with shapes that remained consistent
across his collections. The Spanish designer's

'Delphos' gowns, made of pleated silk in subtle
colours, revolutionized the fashion world. The
elegance and refinement of his 'Knossos' shawls,
his deceptively simple coats and his burnous-style
cloaks charmed many generations of clients.
Immortalized in literature through the work of
Marcel Proust, Fortuny's designs transformed the
women who wore them into characters in a novel.
The decorative pieces that he designed created an
environment shaped by fashion and inspiration,
which refused to conform to the conventions
of the day.

It seems that Alaïa was fascinated by the
all-encompassing nature of Fortuny's artistic
work. The principles that drove the Spanish
designer, who reworked the same forms year
after year without bowing to constant calls for
reinvention, also shaped Alaïa's approach, as
throughout his life he challenged the systems
that governed the fashion industry and its
emphasis on churning out designs at a fast pace.
The Granada-born couturier, who also worked
in theatre and lighting design, undoubtedly
influenced the Tunisian-born Alaïa, who had
also moved to Paris from abroad and was
inspired by Fortuny's way of life. The Palazzo
Fortuny in Venice functioned as his home,
his base for creative work and a place to hold
exhibitions. In 1987, when Alaïa acquired the

Fig. 7
Christian Dior, sketch
for haute couture
collection, c. 1950
Fondation Azzedine
Alaïa Collection, Paris

7

cluster of buildings on the rue de la Verrerie in
the district of Le Marais, he moved his studios,
his couture house and his private rooms
there, including his kitchen, and presented his
collections in the grand glass-roofed gallery
that is now an exhibition space.

A number of other exceptional pieces added
to the collection testify to their creators' unique
journeys, as well as to Alaïa's creative vision
and his taste for little-known or forgotten
works. An embroidered velvet coat by **Myrbor**
(no. 90, p. 133) is a good example of this: it is
emblematic of fashions from that decade and
of the work of Marie Cuttoli, who founded the
brand. The House of Myrbor was known for its
embroidery and clothing lines – some of which
were designed by the artist Natalia Goncharova
– as well as for its carpets and tapestries,
which were based on cartoons by a number of
well-known artists, including Georges Braque,
Fernand Léger, Joan Miró and Pablo Picasso.

Other pieces, such as those designed by
Alfred Lenief, who was a pattern maker for
Paul Poiret, or **Callot Soeurs**, a highly influential
couture house of the early 20th century, confirm
Alaïa's tastes as a collector. While he was a great
admirer of the most iconic names in the history
of haute couture, Alaïa also sought out pieces by

more unconventional and independent fashion
houses and brands, whose work was shaped by
the artistic movements of their time.

When he visited the exhibition of **Jeanne Lanvin**'s
work at the Palais Galliera in 2015,[13] Azzedine
Alaïa was outraged to see that the designer did
not enjoy the degree of recognition that her talent
deserved. Historians and curators were all well
aware of how deeply he admired designers who
were known for their masterful cuts, first and
foremost Balenciaga and Vionnet. However, very
few of them knew that he also held this doyenne
of haute couture in such high regard. After Alaïa's
death, when the Fondation began to draw up an
inventory of his collections, many people were
surprised to learn that they included hundreds
of original pieces by Lanvin. His choices allow
us to build up a picture of the kind of style that
he also embraced. The modest, timeless lines
evident in both Lanvin's daywear and evening
gowns favoured restraint over exuberance.
The overstitching and embroidery that were so
characteristic of her work were subtle rather than
overpowering. The fabrics, in her own custom
colour palette, allowed the simple, sinuous
shapes to shine through, while her use of black
accentuated the elegance of the cut. Spectacular

winged silhouettes and panels covered in sequins and glitter lit up her designs, which were popular with a wealthy, refined clientele.

Jean Patou's work does not feature prominently in the collections of French museums, but Alaïa acquired a number of high-quality pieces by the designer. Patou was a contemporary of Chanel, although he was one step ahead of her in some areas – for example, in drawing on sportswear as a stylistic influence. He also designed evening gowns of the utmost elegance and sophistication. Throughout the Roaring Twenties and the 1930s, he designed clothes for aristocratic clients who saw his work as the epitome of French fashion. The pieces in Alaïa's collection confirm this view. They include a number of garments from the personal wardrobe of Mademoiselle Jack[14] (no. 82, p. 143), who was a house model for Patou in the 1930s. Many designs released under the Patou Sport label, which are now very rare and in high demand, have found a home in Alaïa's collection. They show how much thought he put into his purchases, ensuring that they included a wide range of pieces that were representative of different eras.

In his capacity as a collector, Azzedine Alaïa was constantly searching for the next key piece or forgotten label. His collection boasts works by some of the most iconic names in the history of fashion, but also by designers who were just as famous in their time but have since faded into obscurity, which means that it offers a uniquely detailed insight into the fashions of each decade represented.

Robert Piguet, Lucien Lelong and the stunning evening gowns that his wife, Princess Natalia Paley, was often seen wearing in the 1930s, Mainbocher, Molyneux, Raphaël, Lucile Manguin and even Augustabernard, whose uncompromisingly modern dresses are well worth rediscovering… all of these designers were the creators of fleeting works of art that have now been preserved for posterity.

Christian Dior has a special place in Azzedine Alaïa's personal fashion pantheon. When he was still living in Tunisia, the young Alaïa would flick through the pages of the fashion magazines that Madame Pineau[15] had brought back from France and dream about the voluminous tulle creations designed by the inventor of the New Look. When he arrived in Paris in 1956, Alaïa briefly worked at the designer's studios on the avenue Montaigne, but he only lasted a few days. Years later, after he had made a name for himself and come to dominate the fashion industry of the 1980s, he was approached to take over from Gianfranco

Ferré as artistic director of Dior. However, in the end he declined the offer, preferring to remain master of his own destiny, working for his own label, which was growing rapidly. Whatever happened, his admiration for Dior never waned, as is clear from the fact that many hundreds of Dior designs from across the decades appear in Alaïa's collection.

Jacques Fath, Dior's major competitor in the 1950s, also earned a place in Alaïa's collections and archives with his many bold suits, lively day dresses and evening gowns dripping with Hollywood glamour (fig. 8). Alaïa wanted to correct the record, as history had recognized Dior as the premier couturier of his time and relegated Fath to a secondary place, although both designers enjoyed the same level of renown in the 1950s. He visited a number of dealers and auctions in his quest to acquire as many of Fath's designs as possible. Fath's deliberately glitzy creations show that, as well as seeking the perfect cut, he sought first and foremost to achieve a seductive feel. Alaïa's determination to build up a collection of pieces by this couturier, who died tragically young, shows his commitment to preserving the memory of those fashion houses that he saw as his spiritual forebears.

It was the same motivation that drove him to collect the work of two other designers who have sadly been largely forgotten today. **Jacques Griffe** made his name in the 1950s with a style that built on the techniques of Madeleine Vionnet, as he had worked for her as a pattern cutter and become a close friend. His bias-cut, draped dresses display great ingenuity and masterful cuts. Active around the same time, **Jean Dessès**'s style reflected that of his contemporaries, with fine pleats and flowing evening gowns in a range of soft colours that made him popular with a cosmopolitan clientele. Alaïa's collection includes more than thirty dresses from each of these designers, which aptly reflect their creative approaches.

Today, the Fondation Azzedine Alaïa's collection includes many thousands of garments, accessories, drawings and images related to fashion. This total is being constantly re-evaluated as the process of drawing up an inventory of the garments, sketches, photographs and records continues, revealing new discoveries day by day. The accessories alone represent a sizeable collection that one day will allow us to trace the history of the French millinery, glove-making and leatherworking industries.

Azzedine Alaïa wanted his collection to rival that of the most prestigious museums. Starting in the 1960s and gaining momentum in the

8

Fig. 8
Jacques Fath, sketch
for autumn–winter
1952–53 collection.
Fondation Azzedine
Alaïa Collection, Paris

no. 134
Yohji Yamamoto
Dress
Ready-to-wear,
summer 2008
Black chiffon.
FAA.YAM.0002

1980s, he proved to be a formidable opponent, outbidding foreign buyers. He stopped at nothing to keep important items of fashion heritage on French soil when fashion museums were unable to acquire them themselves.

Alaïa liked to collect works by the most iconic names in the history of fashion, from the founders of haute couture who created the discipline in the 19th century to the masters that he most admired, but all designers mattered to him, whatever their influence and reputation, including his contemporaries.

That is why the foundation has a section dedicated to contemporary designers, which bolstered the collections with new acquisitions that Alaïa had set his heart on buying. He was knowledgeable about designers active after 1960 and greatly admired the work of Pierre Cardin, who was a skilful tailor like himself.

The foundation also has a significant number of pieces from the different creative periods of Yves Saint Laurent and Rudi Gernreich, whose work was a subject of great fascination for Alaïa.

The work of Thierry Mugler, who encouraged Alaïa in the early days of his career and for whom he designed a celebrated series of tuxedo jackets, is particularly well represented. There are a number of Jean Paul Gaultier's innovative and iconoclastic designs, from his ready-to-wear lines and haute couture collections. John Galliano and Vivienne Westwood, who attended Alaïa's runway shows at the rue de la Verrerie, also feature prominently. The collection of work by contemporary designers also boasts pieces by Martin Margiela and Nicolas Ghesquière, who was a close friend of Alaïa's.

But it is the work of a group of Japanese designers that best embodies the more recent, avant-garde movements represented in the collection. Alaïa was often seen sitting in the front row at the runway shows of Issey Miyake, Yohji Yamamoto, Rei Kawakubo for Comme des Garçons and Junya Watanabe, and he was also a great collector of their work.

Film directors are unlikely to be very successful if they are not also film lovers. The same is true of writers who are not great readers. In fact, it would be suspicious if they admitted to this lack of interest. However, from its earliest days, the fashion industry has consistently sought to break away from the past. It may occasionally be used as a source of inspiration, but it is often seen as nothing more than a pattern from which to create something new. In some decades, such as the futurist 1960s, the fashion world turned its back on the past entirely. While designers such as Jeanne Lanvin and Christian Dior said that they

1141

1142

1143

1144

1145

1147

1148

1146

drew on certain shapes from earlier centuries, it would not be until the 1980s and 1990s that a generation of designers emerged, such as Vivienne Westwood, John Galliano and Christian Lacroix, who loudly proclaimed that they were inspired by the past, both ancient and recent.

Despite this inspiration, however, there are no other designers who were truly prolific collectors within their own discipline. Cristóbal Balenciaga acquired a few 19th-century garments, fabric and embroidery samples, as well as a range of traditional costumes, but taken as a whole they are no match for a major collection. Hubert de Givenchy played a vital role in preserving the works of Schiaparelli and Balenciaga, but he had no aspirations to build up a broader archive.

Azzedine Alaïa was the only one to amass a collection of such a scale that it could bear comparison with that of a museum. None of his contemporaries were prepared to tackle such a task. Many of them would have been worried about being buried under the weight of it and becoming lost in the past, with their own work therefore becoming outdated. By contrast, Alaïa launched himself into this mission, confident that a better understanding of the past would inform his own designs.

It is very impressive that a young boy, who came from a modest background in Tunis, was able to work his way up to become a great Parisian couturier – and not only that, but he also became the only designer to build up such a vast collection of fashion heritage. However, Azzedine Alaïa was not satisfied with amassing the greatest private fashion collection in the world. He also welcomed anyone who had personal memories of the fashion industry or family ties, not hesitating to offer them a role working alongside him. One of Alaïa's sales team was the niece of Mademoiselle Renée, who had been Balenciaga's studio director. Marie-Andrée Jouve, who had been in charge of the Spanish couturier's archives, also found a position with Alaïa. Bettina (fig. 9), who had been a famous model in the 1950s, was named an ambassador and friend of the fashion house.[16] In gathering these people around him, Alaïa surrounded himself with stories from the glory days of these historic studios, the kinds of memories that were not always set down in history books but that gave an insight into their ways of working and their creative vision. He became friends with experts and dealers – Françoise Sternbach, Françoise Auguet, Titi Halle and Didier Ludot, to name just a few. Exhibition curators and museum directors were at times his competitors seeking to acquire a rare piece at auction, but at other times they were friends engaging in fierce debates about the world of fashion. Around the kitchen table, as guests started to drift away one by one, these friends stayed behind to talk about their shared history. Azzedine Alaïa's well of anecdotes never ran dry. He was constantly telling stories that conveyed his passion for these designers, whether they were famous names or long forgotten. He always sought refuge in learning from clothes. Whether they were haute couture, ready-to-wear or everyday clothes, military uniforms or high performance wear, all garments had their own lessons to offer.

1
Henri Matisse designed the costumes and sets for Léonide Massine's ballet adaptation of Igor Stravinsky's tone poem *The Song of the Nightingale*, which premiered on 2 February 1920 at the Opéra de Paris. Alaïa acquired some dancers' costumes from the show (see pp. 208–11).

2
'Une leçon de drapé signée Alaïa', *Jardin des modes*, no. 74, April 1984.

3
Some of Madeleine Vionnet's dresses were so complicated that clients sometimes had to come back to the studio and ask someone to show them how to put them on by themselves.

4
Jacqueline Demornex, *Madeleine Vionnet*, Paris: Éditions du Regard, 1990.

5
'Madeleine Vionnet: L'art de la couture', 29 June–22 September 1991.

6
After launching her first collection in 1934 under the name Alix, in 1942 Germaine Émilie Krebs founded her label Grès, a partial anagram of her husband Serge's name.

7
'Madame Grès: La couture à l'oeuvre', 25 March–24 July 2011.

8
Récital des danses d'outre-mer was a series of scenes choreographed by the playwright Henri-René Lenormand, which was performed at the Iéna Room on 2 February 1943. The costumes were very different from Grès's iconic draped designs. They drew inspiration from South-East Asia, particularly Cambodia.

9
Elsa Schiaparelli's evening gowns were unique in that they made no attempt to conceal the plastic zips that formed their fastenings. This subversive feature was a hallmark of the couturier's designs. Alaïa also made his name designing iconic jersey or denim dresses that featured wrap-around metal zips. A famous scene in Marcel Carné's 1938 film *Hôtel du Nord* shows Arletty slowly unzipping a dress, which became a source of inspiration for Alaïa.

10
The sale, held on 3 July 2009 and overseen by Chombert & Sternbach, included 320 lots.

11
The sale, which was held on 10 and 11 May 2005 and overseen by antique clothing dealer Françoise Auguet, included 532 lots.

12
A *visite* was a type of short coat designed to accommodate a bustle, covering the bodice.

13
'Jeanne Lanvin', 8 March–23 August 2015.

14
The sale of Mademoiselle Jack's personal wardrobe was held on 4 July 2011 and overseen by Chombert & Sternbach.

15
Madame Pineau was the French midwife who was present at Azzedine Alaïa's birth. It was she who introduced him to the world of art and fashion.

16
Bettina Grazziani gave Alaïa her personal collection of fashion photographs, taken by photographers such as Henry Clarke, Irving Penn and Richard Avedon.

Bess

3653

Bess

all over the pla

A LOVE OF AMERICAN STYLE

Ariel Stark-Ferré

Azzedine Alaïa's personal collection not only traces the history of fashion, but also tells a story of craftsmanship. From the late 1960s onwards, he acquired and preserved an impressive number of designs by renowned couturiers on the French fashion scene, such as Christian Dior and Cristóbal Balenciaga, as well as works by lesser-known or forgotten designers, from both France and abroad.

One of the distinctive features of this collection is that it includes pieces by some of the most influential American designers of the 20th century. Alaïa acquired iconic pieces by Rudi Gernreich, the avant-garde Austrian-born American designer who was a pioneer of unisex clothing, and by Chicago native Mainbocher, who founded his label in Paris in 1929, drawing in a wealthy, loyal clientele that included many famous faces.

Alaïa was not only a designer, but also a fashion historian. From a very early stage, he showed a particular interest in three trailblazing American designers in particular: Claire McCardell (1905–58), Charles James (1906–78) and Gilbert Adrian (1903–59).

What drove him to collect so many pieces by these designers? While all three were the subject of major retrospectives and exhibitions in the United States,[1] they were largely ignored

by fashion institutions in France and the rest of Europe. The exhibition at the Palais Galliera is therefore an opportunity to showcase the work of these American designers who were instrumental in shaping the course of fashion history.

Claire McCardell and the art of collaboration

At first glance, the Claire McCardell designs acquired by Alaïa seem radically different from the fashions that were popular in the 1940s, such as the distinctive, wide-shouldered silhouette of Elsa Schiaparelli's jackets or the perfectly sculpted bodices of Christian Dior's cocktail dresses. McCardell used humble fabrics such as jersey and calico, even for evening dresses, and did not rely on darts or other technical or structural elements, such as integrated boning, slips and half-slips – an approach that was highly innovative in the 1940s and 1950s, and would not become widespread until the 1960s.

However, as soon as they were being worn by a model, these pieces clearly had nothing in common with mass-produced dresses or ready-to-wear designs. Their pared-back sophistication shone through. They were practical enough to be worn in everyday life and were highly versatile thanks to ingenious structural elements: for example, a two-metre-long sash that could be wrapped around the torso in whatever style the wearer preferred, or a cleverly concealed adjustable elasticated band around the waist.

McCardell learned the art of cutting and draping by studying the masters of French haute couture while she was at university in Paris in the 1920s. She went to sample sales and bought Madeleine Vionnet dresses at significantly reduced prices so that she could study how they were constructed, and Vionnet's techniques had a profound influence on her pared-back style.[2] In 1930, she was given a job as an assistant designer at the clothing manufacturer Townley Frocks, where she began to develop some of her signature styles. She was one of the first U.S. fashion designers to have her name printed on the label of a piece of clothing. McCardell is considered one of the founders of American sportswear, and she was also one of the first designers to introduce looks such as ballet pumps, spaghetti straps, leotards and separates into women's everyday fashions.

The Claire McCardell pieces in Alaïa's collection include a wide variety of her most iconic daywear, eveningwear and beachwear designs from the 1940s and 1950s. Alaïa sometimes bought a number of identical pieces – such as a voluminous belted day coat with dolman sleeves, made of textured cotton, which was very characteristic of McCardell's style – perhaps to study the subtleties of their construction, or simply because he wanted to preserve them for posterity. But some of the most interesting pieces in the collection testify to a very fruitful collaboration between McCardell and the company Fuller Fabrics in 1955.

In August 1956, the Museum of Modern Art in New York held an exhibition in partnership with the magazine *American Fabrics*, which aimed to show 'the tremendous scope, quality, and beauty American textiles have attained in the last decade'.[3] It featured a series of printed cottons produced by Fuller Fabrics, called the 'Modern Masters Series', with a range of patterns designed by some of the most famous European artists of the 20th century: Pablo Picasso, Fernand Léger, Joan Miró and Marc Chagall. Alaïa acquired a number of designs that were born out of this collaboration, including a fabric with a print motif by Léger, which was used for a swimming costume and a pair of voluminous cotton bloomers, an evening gown printed with the same 'Parade Sauvage' motif in a different colourway (no. 23, p. 81), and a single-breasted day coat in printed cotton with a design by Miró.

McCardell was asked to design a full range of leisurewear using these cottons produced by Fuller Fabrics. In November 1955, *Life* magazine published a series of photographs of her designs, worn by models posing with the famous artists

who had inspired them, offering a rare glimpse into their studios and homes. Sally Kirkland, a fashion journalist for *Life*, wrote that the French model Bettina was instrumental in setting up the shoot, especially in getting Picasso to agree to appear (fig. 2), as he rarely posed for photographers.[4] It was Bettina's enthusiasm for McCardell's designs that convinced Picasso to take part, which also encouraged the other artists.

The article, one of the first of its kind, revealed the richness of this collaboration, which brought together modern art, fabric design and McCardell's revolutionary American sportswear. The designer's work with Fuller Fabrics was a way of making art 'accessible' to a wider public, as the dress was sold for only $60 on the U.S. market. Created a decade before Yves Saint Laurent launched his Mondrian-inspired shift dress in France, these designs are a landmark among the myriad artistic collaborations that have shaped the fashion industry from the mid-1960s up until the present day.

A journey in sketches: the foundation's Adrian collection

Azzedine Alaïa said of Adrian: 'For me, he is one of the most important American couturiers.'[5] The sheer number of pieces by Adrian that feature in his collection show how greatly he admired this designer, who started out as a costume designer in Hollywood before setting up his own fashion label. Alaïa bought most of the pieces from an Adrian specialist, Joseph Simms, who founded the Adrian Preservation Society, an organization that aims to preserve and promote the famous American designer's legacy, in Philadelphia in 1969. However, even after this major acquisition, Alaïa continued to seek out Adrian's work. His collection, which features more than 250 pieces of clothing and 1,100 documents, including original photographs, drawings and press articles, rivals that of many American museums.

Adrian, also known as Gilbert Adrian, made his name in the fashion world as head costume designer at Metro-Goldwyn-Mayer Studios (MGM), where he worked from the late 1920s until 1941. He created some of the most memorable costumes ever seen on film during the Golden Age of Hollywood, including the extravagant embroidered ensemble worn by Greta Garbo in *Mata Hari* (1931), which is believed to have taken six weeks to make, the influential frilled gown worn by Joan Crawford in *Letty Lynton* (1932), and Dorothy's checked gingham dress and sequinned ruby slippers, worn by Judy Garland in *The Wizard of Oz* (1939). He left MGM Studios during the Second World War to launch his own line, Adrian Ltd, in Beverly Hills, California, and his designs would go on to be sold

Previous pages:
Fig. 1
Adrian, sketch for the 1948 couture 'Fringe Collection', with fabric swatch attached. Fondation Azzedine Alaïa Collection, Paris

Opposite:
Fig. 2
Bettina wearing an ensemble by McCardell, with Pablo Picasso at the villa La Californie, Cannes, 1955. Photograph by Mark Shaw for *Life* magazine

2

in many department stores across the country. The signature V-shaped silhouette of his suits and dresses, which had exaggerated shoulders and a nipped-in waist, became one of the most popular styles in American women's fashion until the emergence of Dior's New Look in 1947.

Looking at Adrian's and Alaïa's designs side by side, we can see a number of similarities, particularly in their meticulous approach to suit tailoring, which contrasted with the light, floaty feel of their eveningwear. This dialogue between the two designers' work was explored for the first time in the exhibition 'Adrian and Alaïa: The Art of the Suit', held at the Fondation in 2019.[6] While that exhibition focused mainly on the suits that had made Adrian's reputation in the American fashion world of the 1940s,[7] the pieces chosen for the exhibition 'Azzedine Alaïa: A Couturier's Collection' celebrate his talent as a designer of evening gowns. The selection highlights some of the stylistic features that made Adrian's name: a draped evening gown made of purple silk crepe, embellished with a subtle touch of fuchsia inside the bodice (no. 12), which shows his love of bold colour combinations; two pared-back, elegant evening gowns made of black silk crepe, a design that always featured in multiple iterations in each of Adrian's collections. His passion for animals shines through in an evening gown,

also made of black silk crepe, with a printed motif of interlinked monkeys across the bodice (no. 13, p. 76). His meticulous embroidery work, a good example of which featured in an advert that appeared in *Vogue* in 1945, evokes his Hollywood costume designs.

One of Adrian's last requests to his wife Janet Gaynor and longtime business partner Woody Feurt was that all of his original sketches should be destroyed[8] – perhaps because throughout his career he had always been afraid of being copied. It was therefore widely believed that most of these had been lost, until Simms founded the Adrian Preservation Society in the 1970s and managed to acquire some, with the help of Adrian's sister Beatrice Leventhal and Hannah Lindfors, who had worked for him at MGM.[9] These precious sketches, which Alaïa bought from Simms along with the garments designed by Adrian, have since been preserved in the foundation's collection. They offer a rare insight into the American designer's creative process and the unique features of his sketches (fig. 4).

These sketches are usually accompanied by a number and the name of the model who was used to create the toile prototype – for example, Bess, who often took part in Adrian's runway shows (figs. 1 and 3). The fabric swatch pinned to the top of the sketch gives us information about

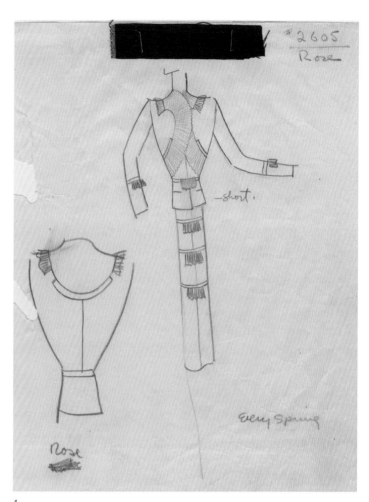

3

4

what the original toile might have looked like, compared to the black wool version presented in the exhibition. The way that Adrian broke down the process of constructing a piece of clothing and its silhouette is particularly interesting. It means that we can see the piece in its entirety, but our eye is also drawn to a specific detail – in this case, the back. Adrian often added theatrical or humorous comments to his designs (fig. 3), and some of his later collections still bear the influence of his earlier role as a costume designer at MGM.

While a comparison of Adrian's and Alaïa's designs highlights their stylistic differences, it also shows that the two designers, who rarely made drastic changes to their signature silhouette and style from one collection to the next, shared the same philosophy when it came to fashion. As Adrian very eloquently put it in an interview in 1950, it is 'easy for a designer to create unusual and amusing new clothes with a certain shock value… the difficulty is in restraint.'[10]

The one and only Charles James

It should come as no surprise that some of the most innovative and distinctive designs in Azzedine Alaïa's collection are by Charles James, a couturier who was once dubbed 'the poet laureate of American fashion'[11] by photographer Bill Cunningham. Although there are not as many pieces by James as there are by other designers, those that do feature offer a clear vision of his unique skillset.

Charles James was one of the most celebrated designers in American fashion, thanks to his innovative approach to cut and construction and his unconventional use of fabrics. Balenciaga said that he was 'not only the greatest American couturier, but the world's best and only dressmaker who has raised it from an applied art form to a pure art form.'[12] James burst onto the New York fashion scene with his 'Taxi' dress of 1929 – a bias-cut evening gown with a zip that formed a long spiral around the body. In an article in the magazine *La Mode en peinture* (1989), Alaïa cited it as one of the designs that he would most like to add to his personal collection.[13] Despite his volatile personality and constant financial troubles, James enjoyed a long career with the support of his loyal clients, who were mainly drawn from the ranks of high society. They included Millicent Rogers, the granddaughter of the Standard Oil magnate, and Austine McDonnell Hearst, wife of the newspaper editor William Randolph Hearst. James's regular customers wore his designs to some of the highest-profile New York events of the 1950s. Alaïa acquired a similar dress to the one worn by Barbara Cushing Mortimer Paley,

Fig. 3
Adrian, sketch for
couture collection, *c.* 1950.
Fondation Azzedine
Alaïa Collection, Paris

Fig. 4
Adrian, sketch for 1950
couture collection, with
fabric swatch attached.
Fondation Azzedine Alaïa
Collection, Paris

Fig. 5
Models wearing gowns by
Charles James, New York,
1950. Photograph by Eliot
Elisofon for *Life* magazine

5

the wife of William S. Paley, founder of CBS, in a photograph by John Rawlings that was published in *Vogue* on 1 November 1950. This design boasted a full cotton petticoat with sunray pleats that contrasted with the velvet and duchesse satin of the dress (no. 10, p. 73). It also featured in photographs of the 1950 Met Gala (fig. 5), taken by Eliot Elisofon and published in *Life* magazine. Bill Cunningham said that he had seen this dress for the first time when it was worn by the entertainer Gypsy Rose Lee, whom he compared to 'a Boldini portrait from the Belle Époque'.[14]

The pieces by James that Alaïa chose for his collection reflect his deep appreciation for the Anglo-American designer's skill in constructing evening gowns and coats. The pieces featured in the exhibition (nos. 10 and 60) are some of the best examples of James's avant-garde approach to cut and his unconventional use of fabrics.

Unlike the world of French haute couture, which was heavily subsidized by the state, the U.S. fashion market in the mid-20th century did not have sufficient financial support, so designers had to make their offerings more commercial in order to survive.[15] Therefore, despite his misgivings, James sold his designs to established brands – for example, in the mid-1950s he designed a number of coats for the clothing manufacturer William S. Popper.

The Charles James coat in this exhibition (no. 60, p. 42) has large, loose gathers at the waist to give it structure. It has three large buttons down the front and the waist is shaped by dramatically curved boning. This design not only displays James's mastery of cut, but also the manufacturer's attention to detail in creating this commercially available piece. The ready-to-wear lines that James designed for William S. Popper were surprisingly avant-garde and predicted some of the futuristic silhouettes that would emerge almost a decade later in France.

Working within the constraints of a fashion industry that was very different from the one in France, McCardell, Adrian and James had to decide how best to use their artistic skills to make a profit. However, they rose above the noise of Seventh Avenue in New York[16] and made a name for themselves by designing remarkable pieces and throwing themselves into original collaborations that have stood the test of time. Their creations reached beyond the borders of the U.S. and had a profound influence on the fashion world, both in France and internationally, throughout the 20th century. Azzedine Alaïa was certainly right to seek out their designs. Now it is up to the students, historians and researchers who have the privilege of studying this collection to tell its many stories to a wider public.

no. 60
Charles James
Coat
Haute couture, *c.* 1953
Brushed wool serge in
ecru, rounded lapels,
fitted waist. Fastened at
the centre front with large
fabric-covered buttons.
FAA.CHJ.0003

1
Some of the most
significant American
exhibitions include: 'The
Genius of Charles James'
at the Brooklyn Museum,
New York (16 October
1982-16 January 1983);
'American Ingenuity:
Sportswear, 1930s-1970s'
(2 April-16 August 1998),
'Adrian: American
Glamour' (14 May-18
August 2002) and
'Charles James: Beyond
Fashion' (8 May-10
August 2014), all at the
Metropolitan Museum of
Art, New York.

2
In Sarah Tomerlin Lee,
*American Fashion: The
Life and Lines of Adrian,
Mainbocher, McCardell,
Norell and Trigere*,
London: Andre Deutsch,
1976, pp. 218-20, Sally
Kirkland, a close friend of
McCardell's, describes the
years the designer spent
studying at the Parsons
School in Paris. She also
writes that McCardell was
very much against the
American practice of
copying French haute
couture designs, which
was a major feature of the
US fashion industry at
the time.

3
Press release for the
exhibition 'Textiles
USA: A Selection of
Contemporary American
Textiles' (29 August–
4 November 1956).

4
Sarah Tomerlin Lee,
American Fashion...,
op. cit., p. 296.

5
Christian Esquevin, *Adrian:
Silver Screen to Custom
Label*, New York: The
Monacelli Press, 2008,
p. 210.

6
21 January–23 June 2019.

7
There are a number of
examples of tailored suits
by Adrian in the exhibition:
see for example nos. 18
and 19 (p. 75).

8
Christian Esquevin,
*Adrian: Silver Screen to
Custom Label*, *op. cit.*,
p. 186.

9
Ibid.

10
'The Story of Adrian',
The Californian, 1950.
A copy of this article is
held in the foundation's
collection.

11
Elizabeth Ann Coleman,
*The Genius of Charles
James*, exh. cat., New York:
Brooklyn Museum, 1982,
p. 105.

12
Ibid., p. 9.

13
In this article, Alaïa
explains that the zip
dresses that appeared in
his collections in the early
1980s were inspired by the
dress that Arletty wore in
the film *Hôtel du Nord*
(1938), but that he was not
aware of the 'Taxi' dress
designed by James almost
ten years earlier. See
Jacqueline Demornex,
'Charles James revisité par
Azzedine Alaïa', *La Mode
en peinture*, no. 15, 1989,
pp. 68-71.

14
Elizabeth Ann Coleman,
*The Genius of Charles
James*, *op. cit.*, p. 101.

15
From the late 19th century
until the Second World
War, the U.S. fashion
industry was mainly
reliant on large fabric
manufacturers and luxury
department stores such as
Bonwit Teller and Bergdorf
Goodman, whose buyers
came to Paris to acquire
copies of French couture
designs, which they then
recreated in their factories
back in the U.S. A number
of designers, including
James and Adrian, made
clothes for wealthy private
clients in their own
studios, but this was not
enough to keep their
businesses afloat. Most of
them were obliged to
collaborate with major
manufacturers, designing
ready-to-wear lines for
them in order to get their
names into the advertising
pages of American
magazines. For more on
American designers'
independence from
Parisian haute couture in
the 1930s and 1940s, as
well as their relationships
with department stores,
see Rebecca Arnold, *The
American Look: Fashion,
Sportswear and the Image
of Women in 1930s and
1940s New York*, London:
I. B. Tauris, 2009.

16
Running through New
York's textile quarter,
Seventh Avenue was
historically known for its
commercial brands, which
churned out copies of
the most popular haute
couture designs from
both France and the USA.

JACQUES F. FATH & Cᴵᴱ

TÉLÉPH. BALZAC 47-60
5 LIGNES GROUPÉES
TÉLÉGR. FATHJA-PARIS

SOCIÉTÉ A RESPONSABILITÉ LIMITÉE AU CAPITAL DE 100.000 FRS.

COUTURE
PARIS

39, AVᴱ PIERRE 1ᴱᴿ DE SERBIE
R.C. 272.092 B

Le
5
Janvier
1950

Madame Joséphine BAKER

Hôtel Napoléon-Avenue Friedland

PARIS

Chère Madame,

Comme convenu je vous fais parvenir ci-joint la liste
des prix que nous pourrions vous faire pour les robes que
vous avez vu hier et qui vous plaisaient.

Tailleur de tweed pour le voyage	86.000
Grand manteau de lainage gris pour le voyage	104.000
Robe de cocktail organza plissé, fourreau de taffetas	110.000
Manteau de cocktail velours noir, manches courtes, doublé de taffetas	127.000
Robe de cocktail assortie, basques, larges bretelles	70.000
Robe du soir velours noir, décolleté au ras du cou, gros noeud de tulle au genou	97.000
Robe de grand soir, velours noir, garni de renard blanc (fourrure en plus)	154.000
Robe du soir, tunique de satin blanc brodé et grand volant tulle plissé blanc	276.000
	1.024.000
Réduction 10%	102.400
	921.600

En espèrant une prompte réponse de votre part, je vous
présente, Chère Madame, mes respectueuses salutations.

Monsieur ALAIN,

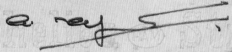

THE VOICES OF INVOICES: ALAÏA THE COLLECTOR

Robinson Boursault

As well as an iconic designer, an architect of clothing and a sculptor of elegance, always pursuing his vocation to create sophisticated garments for women, Azzedine Alaïa was also a collector. Alongside the hours spent in his studio and at the runway shows that made his name, he built up a formidable reputation in auction rooms. His presence there never went unnoticed: the couturier often walked away with the pieces that museums had been most keen to acquire. Alaïa was driven by a single-minded purpose, an urgent aim: he bought clothes to ensure that they would stay together and be preserved as part of fashion's cultural heritage. From one sale to the next, dress after dress, he amassed a collection that rivalled those of the great institutions. Over the course of almost fifty years, he amassed a secret world of treasures, the sheer scale of which remained hidden from prying eyes. It wasn't until after his death in 2017 that the collection was finally unveiled to the world.

The Fondation Azzedine Alaïa, originally known as the Association Azzedine Alaïa, was set up to preserve the couturier's body of work. After his death, it took over responsibility for archiving and drawing up an inventory of his various fashion collections. This vital work led to the discovery of a number of garments, as well as documents related to these purchases.

Sales catalogues, invoices and annotated lists are all important records that require preservation. Together they build up a portrait of Alaïa, not as a couturier but as an extraordinary collector.

For historians, invoices are invaluable documents that allow them to piece together the timeline of a collection. They are an archaeological tool, a source overflowing with clues that help them to put the acquisition in its context, at a certain time and place. The date, address and signature are tiny beacons that allow historians to get their bearings. They use the invoice like a map, to orientate themselves and trace the journey of a piece.

Alaïa was driven by a similar thirst for knowledge. He cared about the context in which each dress was created, the couture house that made it and the person who wore it. He was as interested in the history of a piece of clothing as he was in the piece itself. With this in mind, he acquired invoices listing orders placed by Josephine Baker in the 1940s (fig. 1), as well as outfits worn by Barbara Hutton and Elizabeth Taylor. After the death of Greta Garbo in 1990, he even bought back a coat that he had designed for her.

An invoice is like a piece of clothing's passport. It lists all the important information: what kind of garment it is, the name of the design, its price

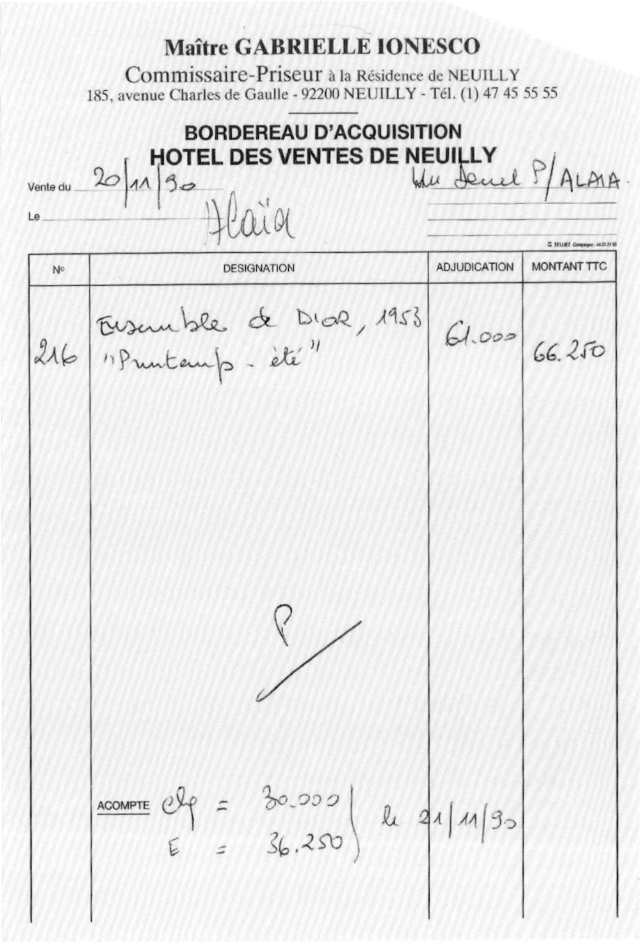

Maître GABRIELLE IONESCO
Commissaire-Priseur à la Résidence de NEUILLY
185, avenue Charles de Gaulle - 92200 NEUILLY - Tél. (1) 47 45 55 55

BORDEREAU D'ACQUISITION
HOTEL DES VENTES DE NEUILLY

Vente du 20/11/90   Vu dcnel P/ALAIA

Le _____ Alaïa

Nº	DESIGNATION	ADJUDICATION	MONTANT TTC
216	Ensemble de Dior, 1953 "Printemps - été"	61.000	66.250

P /

ACOMPTE ck = 30.000 \
         E = 36.250 / le 21/11/90

2

Previous pages:
Fig. 1
Invoice from Jacques
Fath addressed to
Ms. Josephine Baker,
5 January 1950.
Fondation Azzedine
Alaïa Collection, Paris

These pages:
Fig. 2
Receipt, Neuilly auction
house, 20 November 1990.
Handwritten document
recording Alaïa's purchase
of a Dior ensemble.
Fondation Azzedine
Alaïa Collection, Paris

Fig. 3
Sales catalogue,
Cornette de Saint Cyr,
1–2 October 2004.
Fondation Azzedine
Alaïa Collection, Paris

Fig. 4
The Diaghilev and Ballets
Russes Costumes from
Castle Howard, sales
catalogue, London:
Sotheby's, 1995.
Fondation Azzedine
Alaïa Collection, Paris

(fig. 2). The figures and detailed description allow us to identify and authenticate the garment. One example, from the haute couture sale held on 3 July 2009 at Cornette de Saint Cyr, reads as follows: 'Lot no. 97: Balenciaga, haute couture, c. 1945/1950. Outfit for a costume ball, inspired by fashions of 1875, black and cream shot silk, consisting of a bodice with straps and false cape with flounces, a long skirt embellished with layers of black silk velvet ribbon. White logo, black lettering. Valuation €1,550.'

An invoice is clearly a tangible, objective record of a transaction. However, historians are not accountants. They must go beyond this simple reading, which at first glance says more about the result of a sale than it does about the buyer's personality. They must strive to read between the lines, to draw inferences about what is left unsaid, to sketch a portrait of this enigmatic couturier-turned-collector. Invoices are like an open door granting us privileged access to Alaïa's private world. We can trace his tastes, his behaviour and his motivations through the sales catalogues and lists of purchases. These documents become a mirror showing us a reflection of the couturier, his image subtly flipped.

What is initially most striking is the sheer quantity of documents, which makes it clear that Alaïa made a lot of acquisitions, on a regular basis. He kept up an impressive pace, visiting auction houses several times a month, a week or even a day. On 7 October 1997, Alaïa made acquisitions in both Paris and London at the same time. Later, in 2005 and 2009, he exhibited designs by Poiret (fig. 5, p. 28) and Schiaparelli in his gallery at 18 rue de la Verrerie before they were auctioned at the Hotel Drouot.

Alaïa was a familiar face at many major international auction houses, including Sotheby's (fig. 4), Christie's and Millon, but he also bought pieces from second-hand traders, antiques dealers and private sellers who were far from the epicentre of haute couture. He didn't want to miss out on acquiring the ultimate piece, no matter who was selling it. Although his own designs embraced restraint and moderation, Alaïa had the capricious personality of a collector: he wanted to possess pieces, but not necessarily to exhibit them. He may have been understated as a designer, but as a buyer he was compulsive, never missing a chance to outbid a rival or liven up an auction room.

Alaïa's negotiating skills and in-depth knowledge of clothes also led him to work with Maryline Vigouroux to build up the collections of the Institut Mode Méditerranée, of which he became honorary president in the 1990s. For his own collection, Alaïa liked to surround himself

CORNETTE DE SAINT CYR
MAISON DE VENTES

Vendredi 1er octobre 2004
Samedi 2 octobre 2004

Cabinet d'expertise
D. CHOMBERT et F. STERNBACH

3

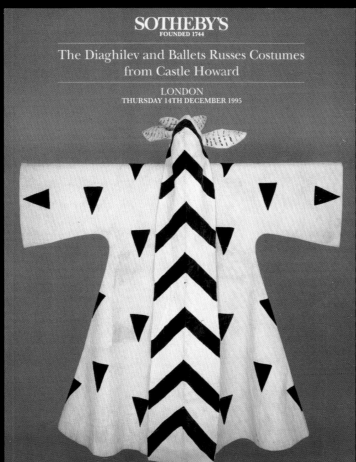

SOTHEBY'S
FOUNDED 1744

The Diaghilev and Ballets Russes Costumes
from Castle Howard

LONDON
THURSDAY 14TH DECEMBER 1995

4

with experts on the history of couture, including Françoise Auguet, Didier Ludot, Titi Halle and Dominique Sirop. As well as business relationships, he forged deep friendships with them, built on a shared interest in fashion and its heritage.

These invoices reveal Alaïa's eclectic tastes, as his acquisitions include works by a range of famous couturiers and little-known designers, across many eras and continents.

His interest in the fashions of the 1930s and 1950s led him to Balenciaga, Madeleine Vionnet and Madame Grès. For these designers, the cut was everything. They placed great emphasis on how they constructed their garments, created volume and assembled a piece – a familiar approach for Alaïa, who had studied sculpture at the Tunis Institute of Fine Arts. Maintaining this interest in proportions and clean lines, Alaïa built up his own personal pantheon of couturiers who approached their work like architects. These great names of yesteryear sat alongside a new generation of designers that included Rei Kawakubo, Jean Paul Gaultier and Martin Margiela.

As well as finished designs, some of the more modest, often anonymous invoices record the purchases of toiles or other preliminary designs. For Alaïa, the toile (a prototype in undyed cotton) for a dress or the pieces that make up a coat's structure were worthy of study, as they offered clues as to a designer's technique, cutting skills and overall approach.

His curiosity knew no bounds. He acquired highly unusual wicker headdresses, silver jewelry and slippers made from plant fibres from places such as Burma, Nigeria and Turkmenistan. As well as fashion, his love of art and design was also reflected in his collection, which is full of photographs (fig. 5), drawings and items of furniture.

When exploring an archive, historians always rely on any paper records that they discover. They comb through them meticulously, sorting them into categories and reading them thoroughly. An invoice is first and foremost a historical document, like a passport or an account book. It provides information about the collection, the main stages of its creation and the major acquisitions. But these invoices also reveal Alaïa's character: not only as the designer, but also as an uncompromising, passionate, well-informed collector, historian and patron.

In the history of fashion, auctions are landmark events, and Alaïa was always at the centre of them. Of all the great couturiers, he is probably the one who bought the most pieces, taking on the responsibility of preserving these designs and preventing them from being scattered and lost. His collection is a tangible record of the past, a symbol of resistance against oblivion, a monument for the generations to come.

Fig. 5
Josephine Baker, 1936, photograph by Murray Korman. Fondation Azzedine Alaïa Collection, Paris

5

THE
AZZEDINE ALAÏA
COLLECTION

I.
THE 19ᵀᴴ CENTURY

CHARLES FREDERICK WORTH

The history of French haute couture
began with a British man, who moved
to Paris in 1845. The career of Charles
Frederick Worth (1825–95) went hand
in hand with the rise of the Second
French Empire. It was an era of luxury
and prosperity, and people flocked to
Paris, the shop window of Europe, home
to a burgeoning industry dedicated to
fashion and style. In 1858, Worth, who
was working as a sales clerk for textile
and clothing merchant Gagelin, decided
to set up his own fashion house. He set
himself apart from his contemporaries
by adopting a revolutionary approach
to design, production and distribution.
He invented the fashion calendar
and seasons as we know them today,
presenting separate collections for
spring–summer and autumn–winter.
He also had the idea of holding shows
to present his designs and draw people
in. Worth revolutionized the relationship
between couturier and client. Up until
that point, designers had been led by
their clients' tastes, creating pieces
to order, but he decided instead to
create new designs based on what the
client inspired in him. Worth wrote the
rulebook on fashion and haute couture,
transforming couturiers into artists, with
clothes as their medium. Like a number
of other collectors, Alaïa was keen to
acquire pieces by Worth. The dresses,
capes and mantles in his collection,
which are made from fabrics in bold
colours and embellished with embroidery
and luxurious trimmings, testify to the
visionary work of this British couturier.

no. 67
Charles Frederick Worth
Evening cape
Haute couture, *c.* 1890
Red silk velvet with
appliqué border of vintage
needle lace around the
neckline. Collar of frilled
black chiffon.
FAA.WOR.0002

no. 66
Charles Frederick Worth
Visite coat
Haute couture, *c.* 1890
Ciselé silk velvet on a base
of raspberry pink satin, silk
tone-on-tone braiding and
twisted metallic gold cord.
FAA.WOR.0004

Overleaf:
no. 68
Charles Frederick Worth
Coat (detail)
Haute couture, *c.* 1890
FAA.WOR.0003

JOHN REDFERN

John Redfern (1820–95) started out as
a draper in the seaside town of Cowes,
on the Isle of Wight. His first suits,
comprising jackets and long skirts that
reached to below the ankle, brought
a new level of chic to outdoor clothing.
Redfern expanded his range of designs
to include yachting clothes, walking
outfits, travel clothes and riding habits,
and opened more branches in London,
Chicago, New York and Paris. His clothes
were inspired by the changing lifestyles
of his aristocratic clientele, since sports
and travel were becoming more popular
pursuits around the turn of the century.
The fashion studio in Paris, with Charles
Poynter at the helm, expanded its
offerings to include dresses, blouses and
skirts, but the brand was best known for
its tailored coats and jackets. The cuts
and colours of the heavy, durable fabrics
used in these designs gave them a touch
of quintessentially British refinement.
Alaïa, who was also constantly innovating
as a designer, had great admiration
for Redfern and acquired a number of
Redfern designs, which together convey
the impressive scope of the brand's
creative output.

no. 69
Redfern
Bodice and skirt
Haute couture
c. 1890–1900
Brick red wool with
braid, embroidery and
astrakhan decoration.
Stand-up collar, boned
waist, fastened on
the left side with
fabric-covered buttons.
FAA.RED.0001.1-3

ANONYMOUS

no. 71
Anonymous
Visite coat
c. 1875–80
Multicoloured cashmere,
flat lapels with plum-
coloured grosgrain tie,
cuffs and hem trimmed
with silk fringing in
matching shades,
decorative bow on
rear. Lining of plum-
coloured shot taffeta.
FAA.ANO.0005

JACQUES DOUCET

Jacques Doucet (1853–1929) is best known for his collections of furniture, drawings and paintings from the 18th century, which he put up for auction in a landmark sale so that he could switch his focus to contemporary art, becoming one of the most important patrons of the day. From 1913 onwards, he filled his apartment with works by avant-garde artists such as Paul Iribe, Pierre Legrain, Rose Adler and Eileen Gray. In 1924, he acquired Pablo Picasso's *Les Demoiselles d'Avignon*. André Breton, his artistic advisor, also helped him to build up one of the most significant collections of art books in France, which formed the basis of the library at the Institut National d'Histoire de l'Art (INHA).

Over time, Doucet's reputation as a couturier seems to have been somewhat eclipsed by his role as a collector and patron of the arts. However, his designs are remarkable for their delicate refinement. His day dresses, négligées and tea gowns were worn by some of the most famous women of the time, from Cléo de Mérode to Réjane. He used extremely fine laces and chiffons in his work, most likely because the House of Doucet, founded by his grandfather in 1816, had specialized in lingerie as well as making menswear. Around 1875, following in his family's footsteps, Doucet opened a ladieswear department, with hydrangea flowers featuring as a dominant motif in his designs.

no. 64
Doucet
Evening cape
Haute couture, *c.* 1885
Moss green plush velvet, collar and hem embellished with ready-made embroidered braid, beaded fringe.
FAA.DOU.0002

no. 65
Jacques Doucet
Day ensemble
Haute couture, *c.* 1900–05
Jacket and skirt. Figured silk satin, sky blue silk faille, woven hydrangea motif in silk thread. Puff sleeves, skirt with train.
FAA.DOU.0001.1-3

BUSVINE

The firm of Busvine was based on
the rue Pierre Charron in Paris, but
the company was founded in Britain.
In London, it was known for dressing
members of the royal court. In the late
19th and early 20th centuries, its riding
habits for women were popular with an
aristocratic European clientele.

no. 62
Busvine
Riding habit
1910s
Jacket, skirt and belt
in charcoal grey wool.
Double-breasted tailored
jacket with fitted waist,
lapel collar, two pockets
with flaps, sleeves with
notched cuffs, vent
at the centre back,
belt, apron-style skirt.
FAA.BUS.0001.1-2

II.
MASTERS
OF COUTURE

CRISTÓBAL BALENCIAGA

Cristóbal Balenciaga (1895–1972) moved
to Paris in 1937 and reigned supreme
over the fashion world for many decades.
His work was shrouded in a sense of
mystery and his designs were true feats
of architecture and abstraction, using
lightweight fabrics to create sophisticated
forms. In 1968, he decided there was no
longer a place for him in the new world
of ready-to-wear fashion and announced
he was closing his studio. Mademoiselle
Renée, his studio director, invited Alaïa
to come and choose any designs and
fabrics that he found inspiring. Alaïa
realized that these creations were at risk
of being lost forever, and with them the
great Spanish couturier's legacy; this
was probably the first time that Alaïa
truly understood the importance of
preserving fashion heritage. The closing
of the House of Balenciaga showed him
how easily this history could be forgotten,
and he took it upon himself to become
the guardian of many couturiers' designs
and legacies. From then on, he was a
passionate collector, not only of the most
iconic pieces but also of a whole range
of documents that told the story of life in
the studios and shed light on the creative
process. His collection includes many
hundreds of major pieces by Balenciaga,
dating from the 1930s up until 1968.

no. 1
Cristóbal Balenciaga
Evening coat
Haute couture, *c.* 1939
Imperial red wool serge,
jet beading and black
twisted braid. Fringe of
black tassels around the
shoulders, three-quarter
length sleeves.
FAA.BAL.0089

Balenciaga, design
no. 106, spring–summer
1960, photograph
from the collection
of Thomas Kublin.
Balenciaga Archives, Paris

no. 2
Cristóbal Balenciaga
*Cocktail dress, design
no. 106*
Haute couture,
spring–summer 1960
Black wool crepe,
round neck, draped stole
attached at the shoulder,
two decorative bows on
the back, fastened with
press studs and hooks.
FAA.BAL.0001

Balenciaga, sketch
for design no. 106,
spring–summer 1960.
Balenciaga Archives, Paris

106.
Taïga

no. 3
Cristóbal Balenciaga
Dress
Haute couture,
spring–summer 1949
Black wool crepe,
stand-up buttoned
collar, fastened with
fabric-covered buttons
at the centre front.
False pockets with flaps,
wing shoulder details,
long sleeves with zips
at the wrists.
FAA.BAL.0016

Opposite, above:
Balenciaga, notebook
belonging to Madame
Florette, *vendeuse*,
autumn–winter 1954–55.
Fondation Azzedine
Alaïa Collection, Paris

Opposite, below:
Balenciaga, sketch
and photograph
of design no. 142,
autumn–winter 1954–55.
Balenciaga Archives, Paris

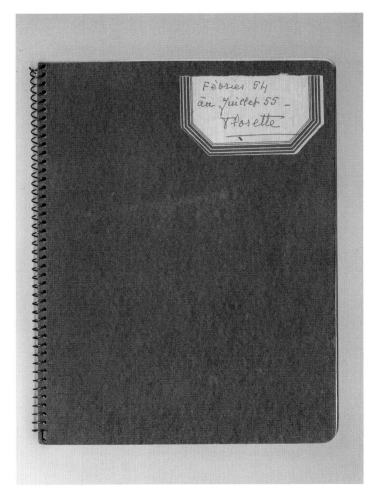

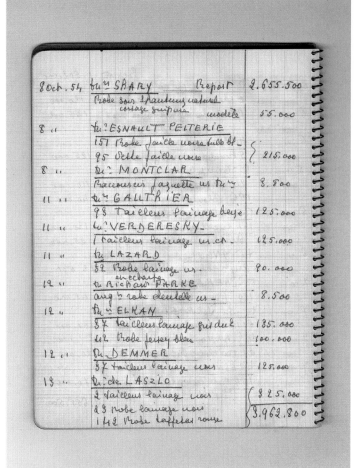

CHARLES JAMES

In 1980, the Brooklyn Museum in New York held a retrospective of the work of Charles James (1906–78), who had died two years earlier. The luxury US department store Bergdorf Goodman invited Alaïa to stage a runway show in the city. During his stay, he visited the Charles James exhibition, where he discovered the complex patterns, skilful cuts and careful research that went into creating his designs, especially his evening gowns. A structuralist before his time, and the only couturier admired by Balenciaga himself, James said he had created only two hundred pieces, which could be combined to produce an infinite variety of clothes. Although he suffered a series of bankruptcies and spent his later years living in very modest circumstances at the Chelsea Hotel in New York, this American designer's work ensured that his name went down in the history books.

Active in London, New York and Paris, James started out as a milliner and then branched out into designing dresses and coats. He created a distinctive style governed solely by architectural forms and deliberately limited the number of designs that he produced. Although his work does not feature prominently in French museums, Alaïa was keen to acquire pieces by James, whom he viewed as a kindred spirit.

no. 10
Charles James
Evening gown
Haute couture, *c.* 1950
Bodice in ruby silk velvet with metal boning, beige silk satin lining. Skirt in crimson duchesse satin. Petticoat in cotton organza with sunray pleats, horsehair, silk tulle and taffeta stiffened with horsehair.
FAA.CHJ.0001

ADRIAN

Adrian Adolph Greenberg (1903–59), known simply as Adrian, began his career designing for Broadway, before becoming head of the costume department at Metro-Goldwyn-Mayer in 1928. His designs were perfectly conceived to look good on camera, and they played a huge part in creating the ideal of Hollywood glamour that had such a profound influence on fashion around the world. His costumes for Greta Garbo were chic and refined, while those for Jean Harlow had a more seductive elegance, and for Joan Crawford, he created a bold silhouette with exaggerated shoulders. In 1942, Adrian left MGM to open his own studio in Beverly Hills, where he continued to design film costumes alongside his work for private clients. Adrian's work does not feature heavily in French museum collections, but in the early 1980s, what is now the Fondation Azzedine Alaïa acquired almost 350 of his suits, day dresses, evening gowns and coats.

no. 18
Adrian
Suit
Couture, c. 1940
Jacket and skirt in black wool serge. Black wool tie at waist. Symmetrical vertical panels of black satin on jacket front.
FAA.ADR.0001.1-2

no. 19
Adrian
Suit
Haute couture, autumn–winter 1947–48
Jacket and skirt in black wool serge. Peter Pan collar with tie fastening, matching tie fastening at the waist. Three-dimensional chequered effect created using folded strips of fabric.
FAA.ADR.0003.1-2

no. 13
Adrian
Evening gown
Couture, *c.* 1940
Black silk crepe with
printed motif of three
monkeys, one holding a
green leaf, looping from
shoulder to shoulder.
Long sleeves, crossover
waist panels, flared
and pleated skirt.
FAA.ADR.0006

no. 11
Adrian
Dress
Couture, 1945
Black and cream silk
crepe, embroidered 'chain'
motif on the chest and
sleeves in alternating
gold and amber sequins.
Fastened at the back with
fabric-covered buttons.
FAA.ADR.0007

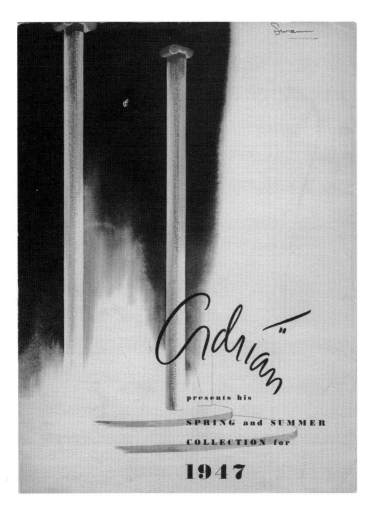

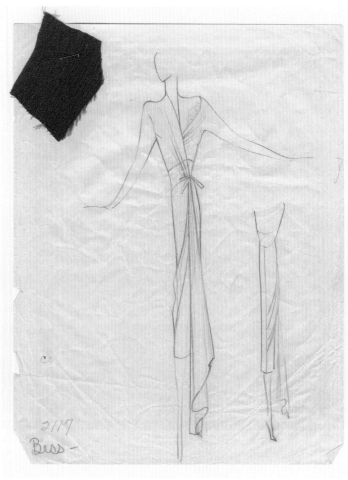

Adrian, programme
for spring–summer
1947 collection.
Fondation Azzedine
Alaïa Collection, Paris

Adrian, sketch for 1950
couture collection, with
fabric swatch attached.
Fondation Azzedine
Alaïa Collection, Paris

no. 16
Adrian
Evening gown
Couture, *c.* 1940
Brick red silk crepe.
Plunging neckline with
wrapover waist, pink
underdress. Asymmetric
sleeves, one long, one
short and draped to reveal
undersleeve with green,
pink and mauve stripes.
FAA.ADR.0008

CLAIRE McCARDELL

Unlike the world of French haute couture, which can sometimes be overly conventional in its elegance, the designs of Claire McCardell (1905–58) are always surprising. Between 1940 and 1958, this American designer developed an innovative style that is now recognized as the foundation of modern fashion design. Her modern approach meant turning her back on many aspects of the luxury industry. She made her designs lighter, with less internal structuring and interfacing, used simple fastenings, did away with linings and used humble fabrics such as cotton, denim and gingham – all functional and aesthetic choices that emphasized her desire to create comfortable, accessible clothes. By designing garments that allowed greater freedom of movement, McCardell was a pioneer of ready-to-wear fashion, which was still in its infancy. Alaïa was fascinated by the effortless simplicity of her wrap dresses and her timeless designs, and he acquired a number of her pieces, the most striking being those made using fabric prints by Joan Miró and Fernand Léger.

no. 20
Claire McCardell
Day dress
Ready-to-wear, *c.* 1948
Grey marl wool jersey, plunging neckline, fastened at the waist with enamel buttons, buttons on the wrist, Empire bodice, inset waist panel, full gathered skirt.
FAA.CMC.0002

no. 21
Claire McCardell
Day dress
Ready-to-wear, *c.* 1948
Red wool jersey, shawl collar, bodice with V-waist, dolman sleeves, two pockets, skirt with inverted pleats.
FAA.CMC.0003

no. 23
Claire McCardell
Day dress with 'Parade Sauvage' print designed by Fernand Léger
Ready-to-wear, 1955
Cotton printed with lettering, figurative and abstract motifs on a cream ground. Lapel collar, dolman sleeves, gathered waist, two pockets. Fastened at the centre front with round gold buttons.
FAA.CMC.0005

CARVEN

Madame Carven, whose real name
was Marie-Louise Carmen de Tommaso
(1909–2015), was a petite, slender
woman (only 1 m 55 cm tall) and was
often frustrated that she couldn't find
clothes to fit her. She therefore decided
to design her own, and her creations
became popular with many women who,
like her, did not recognize themselves in
the affected elegance of haute couture.
She founded her fashion house in 1945,
only a few months after women in France
had been granted the right to vote.
Carven created modern, stylish looks
that were popular with young women
put off by the tyrannical sophistication
of high-end fashion. She popularized the
use of cotton, proving that Paris couture
did not have to use only luxury fabrics.
She was also inspired by traditional
folk costumes and motifs. Carven had
studied architecture and interior design,
which influenced her sense of line and
proportion. She used appliqué ribbons
and carefully positioned stripes to
accentuate her models' waists, elongate
their silhouettes and change the way they
carried themselves. The Palais Galliera
held an exhibition devoted to Carven's
work in 2002. Alaïa's collection features
a number of her designs, all of which
display her subtle and nuanced approach
to garment construction.

no. 25
Madame Carven
'Jamaica' day dress
Haute couture,
spring–summer 1953.
Lemon yellow cotton
poplin with black stripes,
gathered waist with two
small black suede bows,
zip fastening at the centre
front and two bows tied
behind the neck.
FAA.CVN.0001

House of Carven, sketch,
spring–summer 1953.
Palais Galliera, Musée de la
Mode de la Ville de Paris

epuuesroies
rapprochées ds
faille

GABRIELLE CHANEL

Gabrielle 'Coco' Chanel (1883–1971)
changed the course of fashion history
on not one, but two occasions. In 1926,
her 'little black dress' sent shockwaves
through the fashion world, consigning
many venerated couturiers to the history
books. Then in 1954, her tailored tweed
suit pointed the way towards a bold
future for fashion, while other designers
of the 1950s were still stuck in the past.
Alaïa liked to see how he measured up
to those couturiers who, like him, could
master any fabric and use it to create
a dress. But he also admired those
whose approach was very different from
his own, and in Chanel he recognized
a true visionary, a genius who was
ahead of her time and established her
own individual style that went beyond
passing trends. Alaïa's collection of
Chanel pieces includes a number of suits
and coats from her later period, which
display the uncompromising aesthetic
that characterized her work in the 1950s
and 1960s. In addition, a hand-picked
selection of evening gowns from the
1930s showcases the Parisian refinement
of this iconic couturier whose approach
to design reshaped the world of fashion.

no. 58
Chanel
Evening gown
Haute couture, 1930
Apricot silk organdie
with petal-motif appliqué
decoration in the same
fabric. Shoulder straps,
loose bodice, flared skirt.
FAA.CHA.0002

Chanel, 'Dancing dress...',
sketch by Christian
Bérard, *Vogue* (Paris),
October 1937.
Bibliothèque Nationale
de France, Paris

no. 57
Chanel
Evening gown
Haute couture, 1937
Brown silk tulle striped
with ribbons of puckered
bronze fabric. Square
neckline, grosgrain straps
covered in tulle, draped
shawl panel at the back.
Brown tulle petticoat.
Shot silk faille lining.
FAA.CHA.0001

no. 59
Chanel
Evening gown
Haute couture, *c.* 1930
Black silk satin, crossover
bodice, wide back, capelet
with rounded shoulders
and pointed ends.
Circular panelled skirt.
FAA.CHA.0003

GRÈS

Germaine Émilie Krebs (1903–93) first
released her designs under the label Alix
in 1934, then in 1942 she founded the
House of Grès, a partial anagram of her
husband's name, Serge. Over the course
of more than five decades, from the
1930s until the early 1980s, Madame Grès
forged her own path. Her classical-style
draped gowns, her clever pleating and
her mastery of cut and volume make up
a majestic body of work that remains
timeless because it refused to bow to
changing trends. Like Grès, Alaïa saw
himself as a sculptor of fabric, and they
both wielded their scissors with great
skill. Madame Grès's designs, for both
daywear and eveningwear, are difficult
to date because they do not conform to
popular trends. Her colour palette is
made up of deep blacks, chalky whites
and smoky, muted shades. Alaïa greatly
admired her work and sought to learn
from her approach, acquiring more than
700 of her designs. His collection also
includes many hundreds of photographs
documenting daily life in the Grès studios,
some of which were shot by prestigious
photographers such as Robert Doisneau,
Roger Schall and Eugène Rubin.

no. 32
Madame Grès
Evening gown
Haute couture,
autumn–winter 1984–55
Imperial red silk jersey,
plunging V-neck, gathered
panel attached to the
waist on the left, draped
over the shoulders and
falling down the right side
of the body. Peplum-style
bodice, fully pleated back.
Fastened at the centre
front with press studs.
FAA.GRE.0031

no. 26
Madame Grès
Evening gown
Haute couture,
autumn–winter 1980–81
Black silk velvet with
asymmetric cut-out
bodice, voluminous skirt
with pleats at the back,
hook-and-eye fastenings
on rear, horsehair
bands inside at the
back to add volume.
FAA.GRE.0037

no. 27
Madame Grès
Evening gown
Haute couture,
autumn–winter 1949–50
Black silk jersey, fully
pleated front, high V-neck,
long wrap skirt, fastened
at the centre back with
press studs, bodice lined
with black organza.
FAA.GRE.0047

no. 31
Madame Grès
Day dress
Haute couture,
spring–summer 1943
Black silk jersey with
pleated front. Mid-length
skirt, hook-and-eye
fastenings at the centre
front, long sleeves with
pleated shoulders,
symmetrical quilted
motif below the waist
at the front.
FAA.GRE.0014

no. 29
Madame Grès
Evening gown
Haute couture, *c.* 1935–36
Black silk velvet, straight
cut with cutout at waist.
Broad straps, draped panel
attached at collarbone
level at the front and
draped over the right
shoulder. Adjustable
hook-and-eye fastenings
inside the waistband.
FAA.ALI.0002

Madame Grès fitting an
evening gown, Paris,
August 1933. Photograph
by Boris Lipnitzki.
Roger-Viollet
Collection, Paris

ELSA SCHIAPARELLI

Elsa Schiaparelli (1890–1973) was the most surrealist of all the couturiers working in the 1930s. Her penchant for provocative, quirky designs led her to create a hat shaped like a high-heeled shoe (1937), and she also collaborated with Salvador Dalí to create unusual printed motifs. One of her signature irreverent touches was the use of plastic zips, which were meant to be seen rather than hidden, even on evening gowns. In Schiaparelli's work, everything had a symbolic value, like a kind of talisman. Her ceramic buttons and astrological embroidery designs were like protective amulets for the women who wore them. Alaïa did everything in his power to acquire some of Schiaparelli's scandalous designs. Her 'Zodiac' jacket (autumn–winter 1938) and her dress with a motif by Marcel Vertès (spring–summer 1939) are some of the most striking pieces in his collection. He also acquired some unusual documents, such as letters exchanged by Schiaparelli and her secretary during the war, and a batch of toiles from her studios. In 2009, he even held an exhibition of Schiaparelli's work at his headquarters, before a sale of her designs. Among the items on show was a jacket with embroidery based on a design by Jean Cocteau.

no. 46
Elsa Schiaparelli
'Zodiac' jacket,
'Astrology' collection
Haute couture,
autumn–winter 1938–39
Navy blue silk velvet, with embroidery by Lesage featuring twelve gold Zodiac symbols along the jacket's edges, framed with diamante and bands of crushed metallic fabric. Stardust made from glass tube beads, embroidered constellations in diamante and gold thread, shooting stars made of glass and embroidered comets.
FAA.SCH.0001

no. 44
Elsa Schiaparelli
Evening gown
Haute couture,
autumn–winter 1934–35
Black silk crepe and tulle
with a cascade of rhodoid
acetate sequins. V-neck
sheath with apron-effect
front and plunge back.
FAA.SCH.0054

Schiaparelli dress, *Vogue*,
autumn 1934. Photograph
by Horst P. Horst.
Condé Nast Collection

dessin de Vertès
d'apès D 261

no. 43
Elsa Schiaparelli
Evening gown
Haute couture,
spring–summer 1939
Ivory silk satin with print
motif by Marcel Vertès.
Scoop neckline with four
pleats, thin straps overlaid
with origami-style folded
fabric motifs, which
extend to frame the
plunge back. Fitted waist,
straight skirt, bustle and
gathered fabric falling
to the rear hem.
FAA.SCH.0018

Elsa Schiaparelli, sketch
for spring–summer
1939 collection.
Musée des Arts
Décoratifs, Paris

PAUL POIRET

The works of Paul Poiret (1879–1944)
figures prominently in Alaïa's collections.
This includes designs from the 1910s,
which were inspired by the Empire style
and liberated women from restrictive
corsets, and pieces from the 1920s,
which embrace the exoticism that
was fashionable at the time, as well as
children's clothes and textiles. Pieces
that belonged to the designer's wife,
Denise Poiret, including the 'Moscovite'
jacket that she wore in 1913, allow us to
build up a picture of the kind of fashions
worn by an avant-garde woman of the
period. In 2005, Alaïa hosted a historic
exhibition and sale of Poiret's work at
his headquarters, which highlighted the
designer's constant innovation. Poiret
reinvented the role of the couturier
and was the first to launch a range
of perfumes, but it was his work as a
designer that Alaïa most wanted to
celebrate. He was one of the first to unite
the worlds of art and fashion, drawing
inspiration from Eastern art and folk
costumes from around the world,
repurposing and recycling materials in
a way that was years ahead of his time.
All proof, if proof were needed, that
'Poiret the Magnificent' – to borrow the
title of an exhibition held at the Musée
Jacquemart-André in Paris in 1974 –
was a true pioneer.

no. 55
Paul Poiret
*Travelling coat, from the
personal wardrobe of
Denise Boulet Poiret*
Haute couture, *c.* 1920
Cream wool with brown
stripes woven by Rodier,
inspired by North Africa.
High stand-up collar with
asymmetric buttons,
cuffed sleeves. Pongee
silk lining printed with a
lozenge motif and stylized
leaves by Raoul Dufy.
FAA.POI.0002

no. 56
Paul Poiret
Evening gown
Haute couture, *c.* 1920s
Black and ivory silk
taffeta, black silk
organza, appliqué of
guipure lace and beaded
braid with silk fringed
edging. Scoop neckline,
underdress in cream silk
crepe and cotton serge.
FAA.POI.0004

no. 50
Paul Poiret
*'Tanger' ensemble, from
the personal wardrobe
of Denise Boulet Poiret*
Haute couture, *c.* 1919–20
Coat and dress in heavy
brown wool. Embroidered
geometric motifs in
coloured cotton with silk
tassels. Burnous-style
cape with full hood,
gathered yokes at the
front and back, hand
slits in the side seams.
FAA.POI.0001.1-2

Denise Poiret wearing
an ensemble designed
by her husband, 1913.
Library of Congress,
Washington DC

no. 53
Paul Poiret
*'Moscovite' jacket, from
the personal wardrobe
of Denise Boulet Poiret*
Haute couture, *c.* 1912
Green duvetyne
edged with a silk braid
printed with the same
floral motif as the lining,
based on a design by the
Atelier Martine. Wrapover
front in the style of
Russian coachmen's coats,
raglan sleeves, black
and gold braid.
FAA.POI.0007

BRUYÈRE AND JACQUES GRIFFE

COATS

Alaïa was famous for the quality of his coats and suits. During his lifetime, he not only collected captivating evening gowns, but also day coats, which he studied closely in order to learn the details of their construction and design. Riding habits such as the one designed by Busvine (no. 62, p. 63) and cleverly structured coats by Charles James (no. 60, p. 42), Bruyère and Jacques Griffe (opposite) fed into his passion for daywear. As well as these haute couture and ready-to-wear designs, Alaïa also collected a number of military coats and uniforms, which he admired for the purity of their cut and embellishments.

Bruyère, sketch for
the design 'Cristobal',
haute couture, c. 1940.
Fondation Azzedine
Alaïa Collection, Paris

no. 61
Bruyère
Coat
Haute couture, *c.* 1948
Moss green corduroy
velvet, rounded collar.
Fastened with two ceramic
buttons at the centre
front. Two oversized
patch pockets.
FAA.BRU.0001

no. 63
Jacques Griffe
Coat
Haute couture, 1949
Apricot-coloured
needlecord velvet. Collar
with pointed tips, puffed
sleeves, organ pleats on
the shoulders to create
volume. Front fastening
with 22 gold buttons.
FAA.GRI.0001

MADELEINE VIONNET

In the 1980s, only a few fashion historians showed an interest in the work of Madeleine Vionnet (1876–1975), but Azzedine Alaïa played a key role in ensuring she gained greater recognition. In 1984, in a feature published in the magazine *Jardin des modes*, he unravelled the mystery of an enigmatic dress that no one knew how to wear. By carefully studying the ties and fastenings, the couturier decoded the dress's structure. Where once it had been vague and shapeless, it became a masterpiece once again. Seven years later, Alaïa was also involved in the first major exhibition dedicated to Vionnet's work, held at the Centre de la Vieille-Charité in Marseille. Alaïa admired Vionnet for her unrivalled technical prowess. Her work was a source of fascination for him, and throughout his life he secretly compared himself to her. He collected her daywear and evening gowns, made of chiffon, tulle, velvet or crepe, all of which showcased the impressive scope of her skill as a couturier. The magnificent ivory dress from the autumn–winter 1921 collection, embroidered with a frieze motif of horses by Lesage (no. 35; see p. 5), is one of the most beautiful pieces in his collection.

no. 36
Madeleine Vionnet
Evening gown and cape
Haute couture,
spring–summer 1937
Dark blue and blood red
silk crepe. Sleeveless gown
with deep armholes and
stand-up collar. A-line
silhouette. Cape with
reversible hood.
FAA.VIO.0001

Madeleine Vionnet,
sketches by Madeleine
Leduc, autumn–winter
1933–34.
Fondation Azzedine
Alaïa Collection, Paris

112

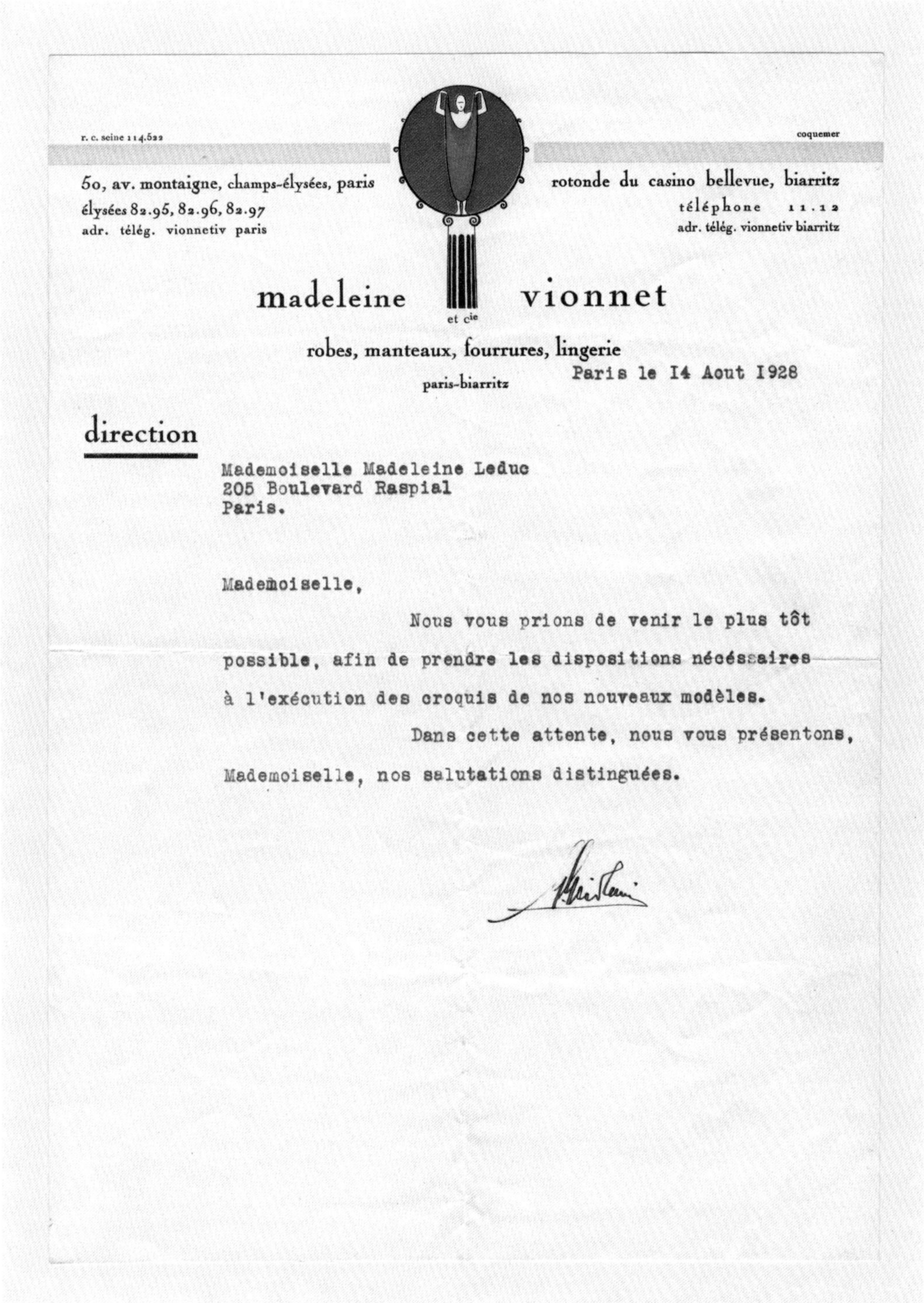

r. c. seine 114.522   coquemer

50, av. montaigne, champs-élysées, paris   rotonde du casino bellevue, biarritz
élysées 82.95, 82.96, 82.97   téléphone 11.12
adr. télég. vionnetiv paris   adr. télég. vionnetiv biarritz

madeleine ▮▮▮ vionnet
et cie

robes, manteaux, fourrures, lingerie
paris-biarritz   Paris le 14 Aout 1928

direction

Mademoiselle Madeleine Leduc
205 Boulevard Raspial
Paris.

Mademoiselle,

      Nous vous prions de venir le plus tôt
possible, afin de prendre les dispositions nécéssaires
à l'exécution des croquis de nos nouveaux modèles.

      Dans cette attente, nous vous présentons,
Mademoiselle, nos salutations distinguées.

[signature]

Letter sent from
Madeleine Vionnet's
studio to Madeleine Leduc,
14 August 1928. Letterhead
logo designed by Thayaht.
Fondation Azzedine Alaïa
Collection, Paris

no. 38
Madeleine Vionnet
Evening gown, design 4271
Haute couture,
spring–summer 1937
Bands of anthracite
grey silk organza and
black silk mesh. Boat
neck, cap sleeves, fitted
waist, flared skirt. Slip in
organza and silk crepe.
FAA.VIO.0007.1-2

no. 37
Madeleine Vionnet
*Evening gown,
design 4558*
Haute couture,
autumn–winter 1938–39
Black silk velvet with
flower-motif panels in
fuchsia, pale pink and
lavender silk velvet.
V-necked bodice,
flared skirt, halter
neck, low-cut back.
FAA.VIO.0008

no. 40
Madeleine Vionnet
Evening gown
Haute couture, *c.* 1933
Indigo silk satin. Boat
neck, draped and
pleated at shoulders,
decorative gathers at
waist. Fastened at the
back with fabric-covered
buttons, rear train.
FAA.VIO.0011

no. 42
Madeleine Vionnet
Day dress
Haute couture, winter 1925
Cream silk crepe, with
nature-inspired appliqué
motifs in black and cream
satin. Pussycat bow and
sleeves with ribbon ties.
FAA.VIO.0010

no. 34
Madeleine Vionnet
Evening gown,
design no. 4113
Haute couture,
spring–summer 1925
Black silk crepe with
embroidery by Lesage
in silver thread and
copper-coloured beads,
filling a teardrop-shaped
panel on the front
and almond-shaped
panels on the hips,
handkerchief hem.
FAA.VIO.0006

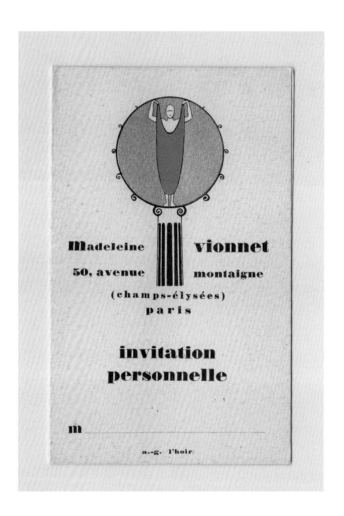

Madeleine Vionnet,
invitation to haute
couture show, 1930s,
logo designed by Thayaht.
Fondation Azzedine Alaïa
Collection, Paris

no. 37
Madeleine Vionnet
*Evening gown, design
4558* (detail; see p. 114)

A DEEPER DIVE

BOUÉ SOEURS

Sisters Sylvie Montegut and Baroness
Jeanne d'Étreillis were born in Toulouse
and founded a fashion house under
their maiden name of Boué in 1899.
Based in the rue de la Paix in Paris,
their studio became known for its use
of lace, coloured ribbons, embroidery
and trimmings, as well as gold and silver
fabrics. The Boué Soeurs' style was similar
to that of Lucile and Jeanne Lanvin.
They also created *robe de style* dresses
with full, voluminous skirts – reminiscent
of 18th-century panniers – which were
an alternative to the straight shift dresses
so popular in the 1920s.

Opposite and overleaf:
no. 73
Boué Soeurs
'Lamballe' dress
Haute couture, 1923–25
Metallic lace mesh,
appliqué in silk lamé
with embroidery, beads
and ribbons. Scoop
neck with straps, wide
belt in metallic fabric
with stem stitch and
cannetille tassels, panniers
on the hips, beaded
fringing on the hem.
FAA.BOU.0001

Boué Soeurs, sketch
for the 'Lamballe' dress,
1922, Boué Soeurs
document archive.
Palais Galliera, Musée de la
Mode de la Ville de Paris

ALFRED LENIEF

Alfred Lenief (1890–?) was an unsung
hero of the fashion world, whose designs
display great refinement and a certain
sense of drama. Lenief was widely
believed to be Russian, but in fact he was
born in Bordeaux. His style was influenced
by Paul Poiret, for whom he worked as a
pattern cutter for two years, after making
his start with Gustave Beer. Lenief, whose
clients included the Russian dancer Anna
Pavlova, represented the new generation
of couturiers working in Paris after the
First World War. He did everything himself
– designing, sewing and sketching all his
pieces while many of his contemporaries
were surrounded by an entire studio
of staff, all contributing their ideas. In
his rooms on the rue Saint-Honoré in
Paris, there was no place for lingerie,
accessories, jewelry or even perfume.
Lenief concentrated solely on dresses
and never presented more than two
hundred in a single collection, which was
unusual at the time. He was obsessed
with achieving the perfect long, slim
silhouette. Lenief also made bold use of
colour and said he was directly inspired by
the sophisticated, unusual fabrics that he
chose. This was surely a creative approach
that Alaïa recognized in himself.

no. 87
Lenief
Cape
Haute couture, *c.* 1925–30
Cardinal red silk velvet,
gold lamé lining. Cut-out
plunging back with tassel
of braided gold thread.
Broad velvet panels in the
same shade of red draped
from the shoulders.
FAA.LEN.0002

no. 74
Lenief
Dress
Haute couture, *c.* 1920
Olive green silk velvet with
metallic sequins and gold
lamé. Sweetheart neckline,
scalloped front panel with
appliqué design in gold
lamé. Welt pockets with
embroidered trim, flared
sleeves and mid-length
skirt in pleated gold lamé.
FAA.LEN.0001

MARIANO FORTUNY

In the early 1910s, Mariano Fortuny (1871–1949) was a true revolutionary, rebelling against the trends of contemporary fashion. Working with a range of simple forms, Coptic or Byzantine-inspired motifs, dyes and sophisticated prints that he designed himself, he attracted a new, refined clientele. The Spanish designer was known for his pleating techniques, which he used to create his timeless 'Delphos' dresses. His 'Knossos' shawls, burnous-style cloaks and Eastern-inspired coats all testify to his desire to break free from the changing trends and constant reinvention that dominated the fashion industry. Year after year, paying little attention to shifting fashions, Fortuny carefully reworked the designs that had made his name. He was also involved in designing stage sets and lighting for the theatre, establishing a pattern of creativity that drew on many different art forms, as can still be seen today at the Palazzo Fortuny in Venice. Alaïa was surely influenced by Fortuny's refusal to conform to the fashion world and change with the times, as well as by the way his creative work and personal life merged together. His collection includes a number of Fortuny pieces that are characteristic of the designer's creative obsessions.

no. 88
Mariano Fortuny
Cape
Haute couture, *c.* 1925–30
Brown panne velvet
with gold all-over stripe
print and stylized floral
panels. Keyhole neckline,
pointed hood with two
toggles and gold braid
fastenings, collar fastened
with six large beads of
varnished wood.
FAA.FOR.0001

MYRBOR

Founded by Marie Cuttoli (1879–1973)
in 1922, Myrbor was a fashion house that
also produced carpets and wall hangings.
Alongside its elegant, unusual dresses,
some of which were designed by artist
Natalia Goncharova, the House of Myrbor
also produced tapestries based on
designs commissioned from such famous
names as Georges Braque, Fernand Léger,
Joan Miró and later Le Corbusier. Marie
Cuttoli was married to the Algerian-born
politician Paul Cuttoli, who was a member
of France's Chamber of Deputies and
later a senator. She established strong
ties between the world of Parisian haute
couture and her workshops in Algeria,
which trained local women in the art
of weaving. Her avant-garde clothing
designs, which combined art and
fashion, remain popular with collectors
as well as museums.

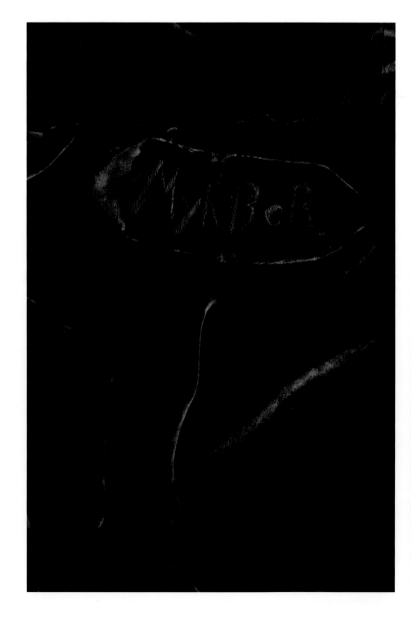

no. 90
Myrbor
Coat
Haute couture, *c.* 1925–30
Brown silk velvet with
panels of geometric
embroidery in gold and
silver metallic thread.
FAA.MYR.0001

CALLOT SOEURS

The fashion house founded in 1914 by sisters Marie Gerber, Marthe Bertrand, Regina Tennyson-Chantrell and Joséphine Crimont, whose maiden name was Callot, had a profound influence on the fashion world of the early 20th century. Their studio was on the avenue Matignon in Paris, but they expanded to open branches across the world, notably in London and Buenos Aires. The daughters of an artist and a lacemaker, the Callot sisters used lace, trimmings and historical fabrics to create an ornate style that particularly appealed to an American clientele. Their designs, which were profoundly influenced by the Orientalist movement of the early 1910s, are undoubtedly worthy of attention. Madeleine Vionnet, who had been studio director at the House of Callot, maintained an admiration for Marie Gerber throughout her life, and said she owned her reputation as an architectural couturier to Gerber.

no. 91
Callot Soeurs
Coat
Haute couture, *c.* 1920s
Pongee (wool and silk)
jacquard with woven
plant motifs in metallic
thread, collar and trim
in blue-purple silk satin.
FAA.CAL.0001

AUGUSTA BERNARD

Born in Biarritz, where she opened her
first studio, Augusta Bernard (1886–1950)
moved to Paris in 1923 and founded her
label Augustabernard. In the late 1920s
and throughout the following decade,
her designs often appeared in fashion
magazines. The couturier was known for
her technical prowess, creating lavish
neoclassical evening gowns cut on
the bias. While her style is somewhere
between Madeleine Vionnet and Jeanne
Lanvin, she was driven by an even more
determined search for purity of line.
Her career was relatively short, which
may explain why so few of her designs
can be found in museum collections.
However, the Fondation Azzedine Alaïa's
collection boasts a few evening gowns
that display her true brilliance.

L'OPPOSITION DE DEUX TONS DE GRIS ACCENTUE LA COUPE SAVANTE DE CETTE ROBE EN CRÊPE LISSE

Augustabernard dress,
Vogue (Paris), 1934.
Photograph by George
Hoyningen-Huene.
Bibliothèque Nationale
de France, Paris

no. 96
Augustabernard
Evening gown
Haute couture,
autumn–winter 1933–34
Cream silk crepe with
mauve-grey panels
creating a *trompe-l'oeil*
bolero effect. Boat neck
and mauve-grey panel
around waist.
FAA.AUG.0001

JEANNE PAQUIN

A contemporary of Jeanne Lanvin,
Jeanne Paquin (1869–1936) set up her
fashion house in 1891 on the rue de la
Paix in Paris. As well as creating elegant
designs, she displayed impressive
commercial instincts and was one of the
first couturiers to expand her business
internationally, setting up a number of
branches across the world. Paquin retired
in the 1920s, and in 1936 Ana de Pombo
took over as artistic director of the brand.
Her suits and evening gowns are highly
prized by collectors. De Pombo made
an impact with her soft silhouettes and
cleverly structured jackets, and it is her
designs for the Paquin label that Alaïa
seems to have prioritized in his collection.

no. 79
Paquin
Evening gown
Haute couture,
autumn–winter 1937–38
Black silk jersey, cords of
braided gold laminette
around the cuffs and in
a vertical band down the
centre front, on a ground
of gathered black chiffon.
V-neck with lapel collar,
full-length pencil skirt.
FAA.PAQ.0002

Paquin dress,
Excelsior Modes,
no. 34, winter 1937–38.
Palais Galliera, Musée
de la Mode de la Ville
de Paris, library

PAQUIN

ROBE DU SOIR EN CRÊPE NOIR FRONCÉ SOUS DE LARGES TRESSES DE BRODERIE D'OR

JEAN PATOU

After presenting his first tentative
collections in 1910, Jean Patou
(1887–1936) moved his studio to the
rue Saint-Florentin in Paris in 1914 and
immediately won over the public with his
sophisticated eveningwear and practical
daywear designs. A true visionary, he
reduced fashion to its simplest forms,
creating entire ensembles from flowing
jersey. His designs featured pleated
skirts, sweaters, twin sets and cardigans
as separates that could be worn in
an endless number of combinations.
This simplified wardrobe paired well
with Patou's Cubist-inspired motifs.
The designer was ahead of his time in
launching a sportswear line, using a
monogram logo on his designs, and
creating a daring outfit for the tennis
player Suzanne Lenglen. Throughout
the Roaring Twenties and the 1930s,
his evening dresses, both short and
long, were the height of Paris fashion.
His work appears in the collections
of a handful of French museums, but
Alaïa wanted to remedy this piecemeal
approach and acquired a number of
Patou designs, which he admired for
their typically Parisian elegance.

no. 80
Jean Patou
Dress
Haute couture, *c.* 1930
Dark blue satin, sleeveless
with asymmetric neckline,
matching belt.
FAA.PAT.0003

no. 84
Jean Patou
Dress and bolero
Haute couture, *c.* 1939
Black silk crepe, bands
of black glass beading
around the waist. Long
sheath dress with boat
neck. Bolero embroidered
all over with black tube
beads, on a ground of
black crepe georgette.
FAA.PAT.0002.1-2

no. 82
Jean Patou
Dress and jacket
Haute couture, *c.* 1935–38
Light blue silk crepe with
darker blue and pink
panels. Boat neck front
and low-cut back, lightly
gathered shoulders,
band of pink crepe with
cut-out motif around the
waist. Short jacket in light
and dark blue silk crepe
with long sleeves and
gathered shoulders.
FAA.PAT.0004.1-2

EDWARD MOLYNEUX

British-born Edward Molyneux
(1891–1974) was originally a fashion
illustrator and trained under Lucy Duff
Gordon, the founder of the Lucile brand.
In 1919, he set up his own fashion house
in Paris, and the three decades that
followed confirmed his prodigious talent.
The silhouette was the dominant feature
in his daywear and eveningwear designs,
but Molyneux also made judicious use of
colour. Many of his pieces can be found
in collections both in France and abroad,
showing that he appealed to a broad and
loyal clientele. His pared-back creations
display a tasteful and timeless elegance.

no. 97
Molyneux
Day dress
Haute couture, c. 1938–40
Dark purple-brown
silk jersey, V-neck and
gathered front, flowing
skirt and deep patch
pockets. Brown silk
crepe lining.
FAA.MOL.0001

RAPHAËL

Born in Madrid, Rafael López Cebrián
(1900–84) was the son of a tailor.
He moved to Paris in 1924, and opened
his fashion house in 1930, initially at
161 rue du Faubourg Saint-Honoré,
then at 3 avenue Georges V from 1939
onwards. Between the 1930s and 1950s,
he presented suits, coats and evening
gowns that made an impression with
their contrasting forms of decoration
and skilful cuts.

no. 94
Raphaël
Evening gown
Haute couture,
spring–summer 1949
Cream silk jersey,
spaghetti straps,
draped fabric over
smocked bodice.
FAA.RAP.0002

LUCILE MANGUIN

The daughter of painter Henri Manguin, Lucile Manguin (1905–90) was raised in an artistic environment. Pierre Bonnard and Henri Matisse were family friends, and Paul Poiret encouraged her to pursue a career in the fashion industry. Manguin founded her label in the 1930s, but it wasn't until the 1950s that the brand started to build a reputation. She showed great technical skill in her tailoring, the way she constructed her coats and her use of soft fabrics, drawing on clever cuts to create an unrivalled sense of volume. Manguin was known for her precision and lack of contrivance, and she also knew how to use colour effectively, favouring muted hues with patterns. The House of Manguin closed in 1956.

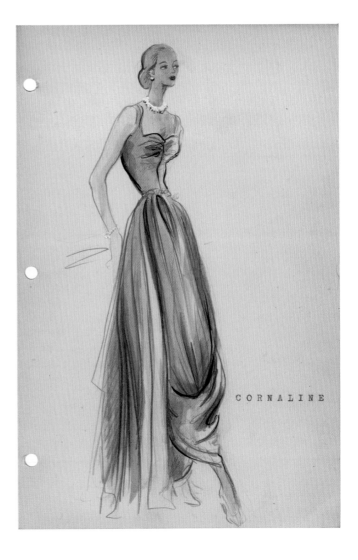

CORNALINE

no. 92
Manguin
Dress
Haute couture, *c.* 1948–50
Bodice and skirt, base layer of coral taffeta overlaid with purple-brown chiffon. Bodice fastened at the centre back with fabric-covered buttons. Buttons on the sleeve cuffs. Asymmetric draped skirt with train attached to belt, bubble hem.
FAA.MAN.0001.1-2

Lucile Manguin, sketch for the design 'Cornaline', spring–summer 1950. Musée des Arts Décoratifs, Paris

JEANNE LANVIN

Jeanne Lanvin's (1867–1946) body
of work is extensive. The major fashion
label that she founded is still active
today, having remained successful
throughout the 20th century. Lanvin
opened her boutique in 1889 and
developed a timeless style dominated
by clean lines, favouring restraint over
exuberance. The embroidery and
decorative stitchwork that characterize
some of her designs are subtle rather
than flashy. Her use of quality fabrics
in a range of muted colours showcased
the simple, pure shapes. Lanvin's work
was especially popular in the 1910s and
1920s, when she introduced the *robe
de style*, with its dropped waist and
wide skirts, to the fashion world. Over
the following decade, she outshone her
contemporaries, designing long evening
gowns with striking cuts, imbued with
classic elegance. Flowing cape sleeves
and embroidered front panels were
among the hallmarks of her designs.
Alaïa greatly admired Lanvin's work and
amassed many hundreds of pieces by her,
which together tell the story of fashion in
the first half of the 20th century.

Jeanne Lanvin, sketch for
the 'Lohengrin' coat, 1931.
Lanvin Heritage
Department, Paris

no. 103
Jeanne Lanvin
'Lohengrin' evening coat
Haute couture,
spring–summer 1931
Copper-coloured lamé
embroidered with chain
stitch in opal green.
Broad shawl collar, full
curved sleeves with
central pleat. Apple green
silk satin lining with the
same embroidered motif
visible on the inside.
FAA.LAN.0003

no. 101
Jeanne Lanvin
'Bouclier' evening gown
Haute couture, 1934
Black silk crepe with
three large gold appliqué
medallions on the chest
and back. High slash
neck, kimono-style
sleeve openings.
FAA.LAN.0007

no. 98
Jeanne Lanvin
'Sarah' dress
Mid-season 1936
Navy blue silk crepe,
hand-sewn with metallic
silver studs and silver
sequins. Draped scoop
front and keyhole back
with loose ribbon straps.
FAA.LAN.0001.1-2

Jeanne Lanvin, sketch for
the 'Sarah' dress, 1936.
Lanvin Heritage
Department, Paris

SARAH

no. 100
Jeanne Lanvin
'Matho' evening cape
Haute couture,
autumn–winter 1935–36
Crimson wool crepe and
duchesse satin decorated
with bands of satin stitch.
Broad collar with large
conical button.
FAA.LAN.0004

Jeanne Lanvin, sketch for
the 'Matho' cape, 1935.
Lanvin Heritage
Department, Paris

MATHO

157

LUCIEN LELONG

The parents of Lucien Lelong (1889–1958)
had owned a fashion house since 1898.
In 1918 he took over as artistic director
and began to put his own stamp on it.
His designs over the next three decades,
from the 1920s to the 1940s, were always
informed by the shape of the body and
prioritized the perfect silhouette. Lelong's
use of black lace and crepe accentuated
the classic, pared-back elegance
of his designs. His ensembles were
immortalized in a number of photographs
by George Hoyningen-Huene and Horst
P. Horst. They stood the test of time,
resisting the whims of fashion, which
Lelong always viewed with suspicion.
During the Second World War, when he
was president of the Chambre Syndicale
de la Couture, Lelong stood firm against
the German occupiers and succeeded
in keeping the haute couture industry
based in Paris.

no. 104
Lucien Lelong
Evening gown
Haute couture, *c.* 1938
Black silk jersey with
panels of self-coloured
silk lace. Sheath dress
with V-neckline and
straps, fitted and draped
waist, full-length skirt
with lace panel.
FAA.LEL.0001

Lucien Lelong,
Vogue (Paris), April
1938. Sketch by Éric.
Condé Nast Collection

Schiaparelli.
Nouvelle version du
tailleur. Ottoman noir.
Noeuds de velours noir.

Lucien Lelong.
Fourreau de crêpe très
cintré à la taille. Imi
tation de dentelle pliss

Eric

Lucien Lelong, sketches
by Christian Dior, who
was then Lucien Lelong's
assistant, 1941–44.
Fondation Azzedine
Alaïa Collection, Paris

no. 105
Lucien Lelong
Evening gown
Haute couture, *c.* 1925–30
Chocolate brown silk
velvet, diamante shoulder
decorations and tulip
sleeves. V-neckline,
draped bodice, buckled
belt in the same fabric
with diamante decoration.
FAA.LEL.0002.1-2

ROBERT PIGUET

Born in Yverdon in Switzerland, Robert Piguet (1898–1953) took over from Alfred Lenief as assistant to Paul Poiret, before moving to work as a pattern cutter at Redfern. He opened his own fashion house in 1933. Christian Dior and Antonio del Castillo both worked as his assistants and he encouraged them in their careers. Piguet's style is an important part of the history of couture in the 1930s and 1940s. He understood his clients and knew that they were driven by the pursuit of elegance, so he created a romantic, pared-back style that was classic and tasteful. As the years passed, it came to seem increasingly timeless.

no. 108
Robert Piguet
Cocktail dress
Haute couture, *c.* 1940
Black velvet bustier bodice with halter strap, low-cut back and boned waist. Luneville embroidery with tube beads and sequins, appliqué design in velvet around the top of the skirt.
FAA.PIG.0002

JACQUES GRIFFE

Jacques Griffe (1909–96) was a close
friend of Madeleine Vionnet's and
worked for her from 1935 to 1939.
In some ways, he was the heir to this
iconic designer's techniques. When
Griffe founded his own label in 1941,
he favoured the bias cuts that had
made her famous in the 1920s, but his
style was deliberately contemporary.
He was known for his draped designs,
his cocktail dresses and evening gowns
with bubble hems, and the clean lines
of his coats. Alaïa was deeply moved
by the prospect of Griffe's work being
forgotten, especially as he saw these
haute couture designs as vital evidence
of the contributions made by craftspeople
and collaborators. This led him to acquire
a significant number of pieces by Griffe,
ensuring that his meticulous work would
always be remembered.

no. 110
Jacques Griffe
Evening ensemble
Haute couture, *c.* 1948–50
Black tulle bustier dress.
Draped bodice cut low
at the back, full skirt
decorated with appliqué
stripes in white, cream
and pearl pink tulle
forming a border and
bow motif at the hem.
FAA.GRI.0002.1-2

JEAN DESSÈS

Born to Greek parents in Alexandria, Egypt, Jean Dessès (1904–70) moved to Paris in the 1920s and opened his fashion house in 1937. Along with Jacques Griffe, Pierre Balmain, Jacques Fath and Christian Dior, he was part of the new generation of couturiers who set the tone for the elegant 1950s. Dessès was known for his draped designs, cocktail dresses and evening gowns made of flowing fabrics in softly blended colours. There are a number of Jean Dessès pieces in the foundation's collections, as Azzedine Alaïa was keen to preserve the work not only of famous houses that were still producing new creations, but also of those that had sadly fallen into obscurity.

no. 114
Jean Dessès
Cocktail dress
Haute couture, *c.* 1958
Black organza, crossover neckline, low-cut V-shaped back, waist accentuated by a belt, full skirt with layered fabric petals over a horsehair stiffened petticoat, boned bodice.
FAA.DES.0003

no. 112
Jean Dessès
Evening gown
Haute couture, *c.* 1960
Black chiffon and
duchesse satin. Bustier
bodice with low-cut
back, draped rear panel,
bubble hem.
FAA.DES.0004

JACQUES FATH

The influence of Jacques Fath (1912–54) on the story of post-war haute couture was profound. His fashion house was founded ten years before Christian Dior's, in 1936, and his ideas were often many seasons ahead of other designers. Dior and Fath dominated the headlines from 1947 onwards. They were often pitted against each other, but in fact their styles shared a certain spirit. Fath was blessed with movie star good looks, but he was also razor sharp, determined and very in touch with American tastes. He was known for his glamorous suits and asymmetrically draped sheath dresses. Bettina, who had been Fath's muse and model when he was young, later became a close friend of Azzedine Alaïa's, and she may well have influenced his desire to build up what was probably the largest collection of Fath designs in the world. Alaïa greatly admired Fath's work and was saddened to see that he did not always enjoy the recognition he deserved.

no. 122
Jacques Fath
Ballgown
Haute couture, *c.* 1940
Brown silk velvet bodice
embroidered with
gold sequins, glass
beads and gold tassels.
Waist accentuated by
an embroidered band,
skirt made up of silk
velvet panels in autumnal
shades of brown, grey,
russet and moss green.
FAA.FAT.0002

plissé

gris

A abac

noir

no. 120
Jacques Fath
Evening gown
Haute couture, *c.* 1949–50
Black silk velvet and
taffeta. Stand-up collar,
buttons at the centre front,
full-length skirt, draped
train and bow at back
in charcoal grey silk.
FAA.FAT.0003

Jacques Fath, sketch
for autumn–winter
1952–53 collection.
Fondation Azzedine
Alaïa Collection, Paris

no. 119
Jacques Fath
Day dress
Haute couture, *c.* 1952–54
Black duchesse satin
with short V-collar, long
sleeves, straight-cut skirt
with asymmetric draped
panel, button fastening.
FAA.FAT.0005

no. 123
Jacques Fath
Day dress
Haute couture, *c.* 1952–54
Black wool crepe
and shot silk taffeta.
V-neckline, five black
buttons, long sleeves.
Straight-cut skirt with
symmetrical draped effect.
FAA.FAT.0004

Jacques Fath, sketch
for autumn–winter
1952–53 collection.
Fondation Azzedine
Alaïa Collection, Paris

CHRISTIAN DIOR

Christian Dior (1905–57) started out managing a gallery and then worked as an illustrator before training in the design studios of Robert Piguet and later Lucien Lelong, where he worked alongside fellow assistant Pierre Balmain. He took the fashion world by storm, creating an enduring legacy in the ten short years between founding his own fashion house in 1947 and his sudden death in 1957. Dior's collections, from the revolutionary New Look onwards, introduced a new silhouette that shaped the fashions of the 1950s, with a nipped-in waist, rounded shoulders and a full skirt that emphasized the hips. He provided women with an elegant, sophisticated look that remains iconic to this day. When Alaïa was still a student of sculpture at the Tunis Institute of Fine Arts, he pored over the architectural garments by Dior that featured in magazines, and when he first arrived in Paris in 1956, he spent a few days working in the Dior studios. Later, his name was once again linked to the iconic brand, although in the end nothing came of it. But throughout his life Alaïa harboured an admiration for Dior, as can be seen from the number of Dior pieces in his collection – more than five hundred. Some of these are by Christian Dior himself, others by those who followed him as artistic director of the house, including Yves Saint Laurent, Marc Bohan and John Galliano.

no. 117
Christian Dior
by Yves Saint Laurent
Cocktail dress,
'Trapeze' line
Haute couture,
spring–summer 1958
Black 'Alaskine' (a wool
and silk serge). Flared
trapeze-line cut, high
waistline with appliqué
bow at the centre front,
fastened at the centre
back with seven black
acetate buttons.
FAA.DIO.0005

no. 115
Christian Dior
'Maréchal' dress
Haute couture,
autumn–winter 1958–59
Black silk velvet with
sash in pale pink
duchesse satin.
FAA.DIO.0004

Christian Dior, sketch
for spring–summer
1968 collection.
Fondation Azzedine
Alaïa Collection, Paris

Christian Dior, sketch
for spring–summer
1958 collection
Fondation Azzedine   Christian Dior,
Alaïa Collection, Paris   sketch, c. 1950.
                          Fondation Azzedine
                          Alaïa Collection, Paris

I

I Tailleur après-midi, boutonnage asymétrique, taille marquée grand col à revers

II Veste tailleur à col long et en pointe, boutonnage asymétrique, forme légèrement en V.

no. 116
Christian Dior
Cocktail ensemble
Haute couture, *c.* 1950
Dress and bolero made
of black silk taffeta and
silk tulle. Bolero with
exaggerated shawl collar,
tied with front bow.
Black pongee silk lining.
FAA.DIO.0008

Christian Dior
Cocktail dress
Haute couture, *c.* 1955–59
Wool, V-neckline with
broad collar, flared skirt.
FAA.DIO.0006

YVES SAINT LAURENT

Yves Saint Laurent (1936–2008) started
working at Christian Dior in 1955 and
became the brand's artistic director two
years later, after the death of its founder.
He set up his own Paris fashion house
in partnership with Pierre Bergé in 1961.
At first it was based on the rue Spontini,
before moving to the avenue Marceau
in 1974. Saint Laurent had a profound
influence on fashion throughout the
second half of the 20th century, creating
an enduring legacy with his themed
collections – 'Mondrian' (1965), 'Pop Art'
(1966), 'Opera – Ballets Russes' (1976)
and 'Picasso' (1979) – and his designs that
incorporated elements of men's clothing
into women's fashion, such as tuxedo
jackets, which he first introduced in 1966.
In 2002, the designer announced that
he was retiring from the world of haute
couture, and an extravagant runway show
tracing the course of his career was held
at the Centre Georges Pompidou. Yves
Saint Laurent's work features prominently
in Alaïa's collection, particularly his
designs that make use of chiffon to create
transparency, exuding a subtle sensuality.

no. 128
Yves Saint Laurent
Evening gown
Haute couture,
autumn–winter 1962–63
Black silk crepe, integrated
bustier in black silk tulle,
long straight-cut skirt
with draped detail and
bow at knee level.
FAA.YSL.0003

Yves Saint Laurent atelier
specification sheet, known
as a 'Bible page', showing
a design for an evening
gown, autumn–winter
1962–63 collection.
Musée Yves Saint
Laurent, Paris

no. 129
Yves Saint Laurent
*Evening gown, design
no. 74, worn by Danielle
Luquet de Saint Germain*
Haute couture,
autumn–winter 1968–69
Black chiffon, round
neck, embellished with
a band of ostrich feathers
around the hips.
FAA.YSL.0004

PIERRE CARDIN

One of the few couturiers who was skilled at all stages of sketching, cutting and sewing, Pierre Cardin (1922–2020) first rose through the ranks at Jeanne Paquin and Elsa Schiaparelli in the 1940s, before taking on the sought-after position of head tailor at Christian Dior. After working on the designs for the New Look collection, which was a resounding global success, he suddenly quit Dior and started a business designing costumes for the stage. But his future lay in the world of fashion, where he would play a major role in the evolution and modernization of the industry. From 1953 onwards, when he released his first haute couture collection, Cardin embraced the popular trends of the 1950s but his designs also stood out as they embodied a more consciously architectural approach. In the 1960s, Cardin's style underwent a remarkable revolution when he presented strikingly futuristic designs inspired by space suits. Thanks to a number of carefully negotiated licenses, the brand flourished and its designs reached the mass market.

no. 127
Pierre Cardin
Dress
Haute couture, 1969
Trapeze cut in black wool
crepe, round neckline,
sleeveless, with pleats
falling from the bust
to the bubble hem.
FAA.CAR.0001.1-2

III.
CONTEMPORARY DESIGNERS

ALEXANDER MCQUEEN

Alexander McQueen (1969–2010) trained
as a tailor on London's Savile Row before
studying at Central Saint Martins College
of Art. He combined masterful, precise
cuts with extravagant designs inspired
by metaphorical and historical themes.
His deliberately theatrical, flamboyant
collections held up a mirror to a world
falling into decay. His work was often
provocative, mocking the vanity of
appearances in a number of runway
shows that shaped the fashion world in
the late 20th and early 21st centuries.

no. 130
Alexander McQueen
Evening gown, look 43
Ready-to-wear,
autumn-winter 2007–8
Black hammered satin
crepe, V-neckline and
train. Embellished with
silver glass tube beads
forming a motif of
tumbling tresses of hair
falling from the neckline.
FAA.MCQ.0001

CHRISTIAN DIOR
BY JOHN GALLIANO

Throughout his career, from his graduation collection 'Les Incroyables', presented in 1983, which was inspired by the clothing styles of post-Revolutionary France, John Galliano was driven by his personal fashion obsessions. A talented tailor, he used his complex bias-cut patterns and impressive asymmetric draped designs to explore historical themes. In 1997, when he was creating the haute couture and ready-to-wear lines at Christian Dior, the British designer imbued his collections with the pomp and exuberance that had been characteristic of the brand's founder. His style was inspired by a range of sources, from 18th-century fashion to folk costumes and urban influences. In 2014, Galliano was named artistic director of Martin Margiela.

no. 135
Christian Dior
by John Galliano
Evening gown, look 46
Ready-to-wear,
spring–summer 2000
Pale blue-green satin with
woven floral medallion
motifs. Unstructured
shape with zips and
cut-outs, pockets and
panels, puff sleeves,
asymmetric hem and train.
FAA.GAL.0001

THIERRY MUGLER

Thierry Mugler (1945–2022) trained as a ballet dancer at the Opéra du Rhin and maintained a passionate relationship with the stage throughout his life. He moved to Paris in the early 1970s and threw himself into the fashion world with the same enthusiasm he'd shown for performing. In 1974, he founded his own label, and three years later, his first spectacular runway show set out a clear statement of intent. His collections were dedicated to real-life heroines that he admired and those he invented himself. The designer had a profound influence on the fashion world of the 1980s. His streamlined silhouettes with exaggerated shoulders created an image of a strong woman, with a touch of seductive Hollywood glamour. Mugler encouraged Alaïa to hold his first runway show and continued to offer him unwavering support as he forged his own creative path. The two designers became friends and worked closely together. The Fondation Azzedine Alaïa's collections include a large number of pieces by Mugler, whom Alaïa saw as a mentor.

no. 131
Thierry Mugler
Evening gown
Ready-to-wear,
autumn–winter 1987–88
Black panne velvet,
draped plunge back
edged with broad pearl
pink satin collar.
FAA.MUG.0001

JEAN PAUL GAULTIER

Jean Paul Gaultier presented his first collection in 1977, having previously worked for Pierre Cardin. From his earliest days, his work was characterized by a deliberate blending of styles and ideas, a juxtaposition or fusion of identities. From 1997 onwards, Gaultier's ready-to-wear lines and haute couture collections adopted a revolutionary approach, making the fashion world see everyday items of clothing in a new light – whether it was a trench coat, a double-breasted jacket, a striped sailor top or a bomber jacket. He inverted traditionally masculine and feminine fashions, confirming his status as a visionary designer who opened up new stylistic avenues for the fashion industry at the turn of the 21st century. Alaïa greatly admired the work of his contemporary and made a concerted effort to build up a representative collection of pieces by Gaultier.

no. 136
Jean Paul Gaultier
Trenchcoat dress, look 19
Haute couture,
autumn–winter 2010–11
Black acetate and rayon
crepe. Double-breasted
effect, lapel collar, storm
flaps on chest and
back, epaulettes and
adjustable cuffs. Buckled
belt made of the same
fabric, miniskirt front
and full-length back.
FAA.JPG.0001

JUNYA WATANABE

Junya Watanabe was initially a pattern cutter for Rei Kawakubo and launched his first line under his own name in 1992, distributed by the brand Comme des Garçons. A brilliant technician who combines experimental cuts and fabrics to create poetic forms, Watanabe has left a lasting impression on fashion in the late 20th and early 21st centuries. His collections are often based around themes, such as origami or zips, and display such great skill and creativity that he could be said to have invented a whole new category of clothing.

Opposite and overleaf:
no. 133
Junya Watanabe
Dress, look 19
Ready-to-wear,
spring–summer 2005
V-neckline bodice made
from multiple bronze
zip fastenings. Low-cut
back and flared skirt
in black cotton with
raw-edge hem.
FAA.JUN.0001

REI KAWAKUBO
FOR COMME DES GARÇONS

Since launching the brand Comme des
Garçons in 1973, Rei Kawakubo has had
a profound influence on the evolution
of contemporary fashion. In the early
1980s, she was part of a stylistic
revolution, reinventing the discipline
of design. Her clothes celebrate a sense
of incompleteness and randomness,
deliberately incorporating holes and
wear and tear to create an intentionally
dishevelled look that opens up new
creative possibilities. In the 1990s and
2000s, her use of unusual abstract shapes
led her designs into uncharted territory.
Alaïa greatly admired Kawakubo and
recognized that the clothes she designed
had a very different relationship with
the body from those that he designed
himself. He collected a number of pieces
characterized by jutting projections and
protrusions, perhaps as a way of better
understanding the curved silhouettes
of his own designs.

no. 132
Comme des Garçons
Dress, look 12
Ready-to-wear,
spring–summer 2014
Tulle, jersey, viscose,
bows and fringing in
shades of black. Pyramid-
shaped framework,
high collar, sleeveless.
FAA.CDG.0001

HENRI MATISSE COSTUMES FOR *THE SONG OF THE NIGHTINGALE*

In 1919, Henri Matisse was commissioned to design the costumes and set for *The Song of the Nightingale*, his first collaboration with the world of theatre. Inspired by Hans Christian Andersen's story 'The Nightingale', this ballet told the story of a dying emperor who is saved by the song of a nightingale. In 1917, Sergei Diaghilev asked Igor Stravinsky to compose a symphonic poem based on Acts II and III of his first opera, *The Nightingale*, completed in 1914. This adaptation, which featured choreography by Léonide Massine, premiered at the Opéra de Paris in 1920.

In designing the costume for the secondary role of a Mourner (or grieving parent), Matisse drew inspiration from the traditional headdresses of the Kyrgyz people, a nomadic group living in central Asia and parts of China. He included a long hanging panel of fabric at the back, which is a feature of the headdresses traditionally worn by Kyrgyz women, and used velvet and felt, the materials used for men's headdresses. In China, dark blue is associated with winter and death, while beige is associated with mourning. However, the headdress's zoomorphic ears or antlers evoke the image of a deer – an animal that symbolizes long life and nature's life force – thereby suggesting the emperor will be healed.

The dark triangles, which Matisse cut out with scissors and appliquéd onto the coat's pale ground, prefigured his large abstract compositions made of cut-out paper shapes, as well as the priest's robes that he designed for the chapel in Vence in the 1950s. Of the ten Mourner costumes worn in the ballet, only five have been preserved (two are in the Fondation Azzedine Alaïa's collection, one is in the National Gallery of Art in Washington DC, one is in the National Gallery of Australia in Canberra, and one is in the Musée d'Art et d'Histoire in Geneva).

For the Mandarin's winter costume, made of silk with cotton padding, Matisse drew on different elements of imperial court costumes from the Qing dynasty. The golden yellow colour, worn only by high-ranking officials, symbolizes Earth, while the appliqué circles of gold lamé symbolize Fire (the sun or moon). The ink strokes, which at first glance seem to depict flowers, also recall the sinuous, concentric lines used in traditional dress to represent the movements of Air.

These unusual and historic pieces were acquired by Azzedine Alaïa in 1995.

Anastasia Ozoline

no. 140
Henri Matisse
Stage costume: 'Mourner'
First performance on 2 February 1920 at the Opéra de Paris
Dress and hood made of light beige wool felt. Hood with long rectangular panel falling from the back, with appliqué chevron motif in dark blue velvet. Bow-style motif on the forehead and two stiff stand-up 'ears'. Trapeze-line dress, round collar, all-over appliqué motif of dark blue velvet triangles.
FAA.BAR.0002.1-2

Of all the costumes that Henri Matisse designed for *The Song of the Nightingale*, Azzedine Alaïa acquired those that were most audacious and abstract. The freeform hand-painted flowers on the Mandarin's costume are a highly modern decorative motif, while the appliqué triangles and chevrons on the Mourner's costume are more austere and geometric, creating a strong sense of contrast and rhythm.

This was the first time that Matisse had agreed to be part of the production of a ballet. Designing the set, the curtain and the costumes allowed him to use his creativity in a new way: 'For me it will be an experiment,' he said. The painter returned to the theme of ballet in the early 1930s when he created his monumental artwork *The Dance*, two versions of which can be found in the collection of the Musée d'Art Moderne de Paris. For that piece, Matisse returned to the technique of paper cut-outs with which he had experimented when designing the set for *The Song of the Nightingale*.

Charlotte Barat

no. 139
Henri Matisse
Stage costume: 'Mandarin'
First performance on
2 February 1920 at
the Opéra de Paris
Golden yellow shot
silk satin, trapeze line,
stand-up collar fastened
with three buttons,
long kimono sleeves,
flower motifs with petals
hand-painted in black
ink and padded centres
covered in yellow and
metallic gold thread,
whole garment quilted,
with cheesecloth lining.
FAA.BAR.0001

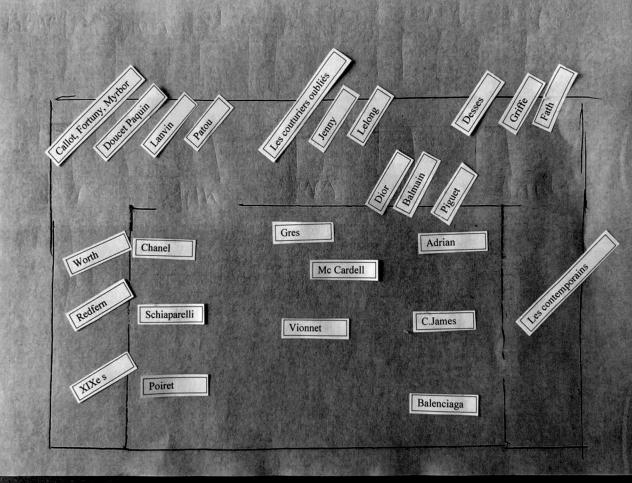

Callot, Fortuny, Myrbor

Doucet Paquin

Lanvin

Patou

Les couturiers oubliés

Jenny

Lelong

Desses

Griffe

Fath

Dior

Balmain

Piguet

Gres

Adrian

Worth

Chanel

Mc Cardell

Redfern

Schiaparelli

Vionnet

C.James

Les contemporains

XIXe s

Poiret

Balenciaga

LIST OF EXHIBITED WORKS

This list follows the order in which the designers' works are presented in the exhibition.

no. 1
Repr. p. 67
Cristóbal Balenciaga
Evening coat
Haute couture, *c.* 1939
Imperial red wool serge, jet beading
and black twisted braid. Fringe with
black tassels around the shoulders,
three-quarter length sleeves.
FAA.BAL.0089

no. 2
Repr. p. 68
Cristóbal Balenciaga
Cocktail dress, design no. 106
Haute couture, spring–summer 1960
Black wool crepe, round neck, draped
stole attached at the shoulder, two
decorative bows on the back, fastened
with press studs and hooks. Black silk
slip with straps.
FAA.BAL.0001

no. 3
Repr. p. 70
Cristóbal Balenciaga
Dress
Haute couture, spring–summer 1949
Black wool crepe, stand-up buttoned
collar, fastened with fabric-covered
buttons at the centre front, buttons on
the back and zip fastening on the left side.
Slits to hip height, false pockets with flaps,
wing shoulder details, long sleeves with
zips at the wrists.
FAA.BAL.0016

no. 4
Repr. p. 6
Cristóbal Balenciaga
*'Mozart' costume worn by Barbara Hutton
to Charles de Beistegui's masquerade ball,
held on 14 September 1951 at the Palazzo
Labia, Venice*
Ensemble comprising a frock coat and
knickerbockers. Jacket in a Louis XV style,
silk velvet with embroidery by Rébé,
Chantilly lace appliqué, embellished
with rhinestones, tube beads and jet
cabochons. Tailored collar, long coat tails,
false jet buttons at the centre front. Black
silk satin knickerbockers in an 18th-century
style, elastic at the centre back and hook-
and-eye fastenings, pockets, tapered legs
with cuff below the knee, fastened with
fabric-covered buttons. Sleeve cuffs in
white organdie and cravat in ivory silk
voile, both with flounces of Brussels lace.
FAA.BAL.0032.1-2

no. 5
Cristóbal Balenciaga
Cocktail dress
Haute couture, autumn–winter 1960–61
Black silk crepe, asymmetric bubble skirt.
Boat neck at the front, draped back.
Fastened with hooks and press studs.
Fabric panel attached at the back and
looped around the front, fastened at
the waist with a ribbon and hook-and-
eye fastenings.
FAA.BAL.0003

no. 6
Cristóbal Balenciaga
*Cocktail dress known as the 'Balloon'
dress, design no. 142*
Haute couture, autumn–winter 1954–55
Black silk taffeta, flat collar with lapels
forming a boat neck at the front and a
V-back. Skirt gathered at the hips, drop
waist and fitted bodice. Fastened at the
back with fabric-covered buttons, press
studs and hook-and-eye fastenings.
FAA.BAL.0002

no. 7
Cristóbal Balenciaga
Evening gown
Haute couture, *c.* 1950
Lace embroidered with floral motifs in
ribbon and black silk taffeta. Fastened at
the centre back with lace-covered buttons.
FAA.BAL.0022

no. 8
Cristóbal Balenciaga
Evening gown, design no. 151
Haute couture, spring–summer 1968
Silk crepe with screen-printed motif
in three colours (green and two shades
of pink) on an ivory ground, straight cut,
long sleeves and round neck. Knee-high
split at the centre front.
FAA.BAL.0081

no. 9
Charles James
Evening gown
Haute couture, *c.* 1947
Striped satin damask in anthracite
grey, bias cut. V-neck with centre pleat.
Shoulder cutouts to create the effect of
four straps, low-cut back, flowing skirt
with two hip-level pleats at the front.
FAA.CHJ.0002

no. 10
Repr. p. 73
Charles James
Evening gown
Haute couture, *c.* 1950
Bodice in ruby silk velvet with metal
boning, beige silk satin lining. Skirt in
crimson duchesse satin. Petticoat in cotton
organza with sunray pleats, horsehair, silk
tulle and taffeta stiffened with horsehair.
FAA.CHJ.0001

no. 11
Repr. p. 77
Adrian
Dress
Couture, 1945
Black and cream silk crepe,
embroidered 'chain' motif on the chest
and sleeves in alternating gold and
amber sequins. Fastened at the back
with fabric-covered buttons.
FAA.ADR.0007

no. 12
Adrian
Evening gown
Couture, *c.* 1940
Purple and fuchsia silk crepe. Deep
V-neckline with pleats, long sleeves,
wrap front with draped panel of pleated
purple fabric, backed with panel of
fuchsia fabric.
FAA.ADR.0009

no. 13
Repr. p. 76
Adrian
Evening gown
Couture, *c.* 1940
Black silk crepe with printed motif of
three monkeys, one holding a green leaf,
looping from shoulder to shoulder. Long
sleeves, crossover waist panels, flared
and pleated skirt.
FAA.ADR.0006

no. 14
Adrian
Evening gown
Couture, *c.* 1940
Midnight blue goffered silk crepe.
Sweetheart neckline, panels of black
silk faille below the bust, finished with
two flounces with broad flat pleats at
the rear waist.
FAA.ADR.0005

no. 15
Adrian
Evening gown
Couture, *c.* 1940
Black silk crepe. V-neckline with
gathered fabric at the centre front
and butterfly sleeves. Fitted skirt
with handkerchief hem.
FAA.ADR.0004

no. 16
Repr. p. 79
Adrian
Evening gown
Couture, *c.* 1940
Brick red silk crepe. Plunging neckline
with wrapover waist, pink underdress.
Asymmetric sleeves, one long, one
short and draped to reveal undersleeve
with green, pink and mauve stripes.
FAA.ADR.0008

no. 17
Adrian
Suit
Couture, *c.* 1940
Jacket and skirt in black wool serge.
Jacket with plain collar, false cape with
short pleated border matching the one
on the jacket's lower edge. Fastened at
the centre front with pearl-effect buttons.
Skirt with peplum-style hem at the front
and box pleat at the centre back.
FAA.ADR.0002.1-2

no. 18
Repr. p. 75
Adrian
Suit
Couture, *c.* 1940
Jacket and skirt in black wool serge.
Black wool tie at waist. Symmetrical
vertical panels of black satin on jacket
front, hidden pockets.
FAA.ADR.0001.1-2

no. 19
Repr. p. 75
Adrian
Suit
Haute couture, autumn–winter 1947–48
Jacket and skirt in black wool serge.
Peter Pan collar with tie fastening,
matching tie fastening at the waist, hidden
pockets. Three-dimensional chequered
effect created using folded strips of fabric.
FAA.ADR.0003.1-2

no. 20
Repr. p. 80
Claire McCardell
Day dress
Ready-to-wear, *c.* 1948
Grey marl wool jersey, plunging neckline,
fastened at the waist with enamel buttons,
buttons on the wrist, Empire bodice, inset
waist panel, full gathered skirt.
FAA.CMC.0002

no. 21
Repr. p. 80
Claire McCardell
Day dress
Ready-to-wear, *c.* 1948
Red wool jersey, shawl collar, bodice
with V-waist, dolman sleeves, two
pockets, skirt with inverted pleats.
FAA.CMC.0003

no. 22
Claire McCardell
Day dress
Ready-to-wear, *c.* 1948
Black artificial silk, deep V-neck, knife
pleats at the waist, Empire waist and wide
inset belt. Flared skirt made from eight
vertical panels.
FAA.CMC.0004

no. 23
Repr. p. 81
Claire McCardell
*Day dress with 'Parade Sauvage'
print designed by Fernand Léger*
Ready-to-wear, 1955
Cotton printed with lettering, figurative
and abstract motifs in shades of pink,
orange and black on a cream ground.
Lapel collar, dolman sleeves, gathered
waist, two pockets. Fastened at the
centre front with round gold buttons
FAA.CMC.0005

no. 24
Mad Carpentier
Day dress
Couture, *c.* 1947–48
Black wool, low-cut neckline with broad
lapels. Cape-effect sleeves, zip fastening
at the centre front and two pockets.
FAA.MAD.0001

no. 25
Repr. p. 82
Madame Carven
'Jamaica' day dress
Haute couture, spring–summer 1953
Lemon yellow cotton poplin with black
stripes, gathered waist with two small
black suede bows, zip fastening at the
centre front and two bows tied behind
the neck.
FAA.CVN.0001

no. 26
Repr. p. 92
Madame Grès
Evening gown
Haute couture, autumn–winter 1980–81
Black silk velvet with asymmetric cut-out
bodice, voluminous skirt with pleats
at the back, hook-and-eye fastenings
on rear, horsehair bands inside at the
back to add volume.
FAA.GRE.0037

no. 27
Repr. p. 93
Madame Grès
Evening gown
Black silk jersey, fully pleated front, high V-neck, long wrap skirt, fastened at the centre back with press studs, bodice lined with black organza.
FAA.GRE.0047

no. 28
Madame Grès
Evening gown
Haute couture, c. 1943
Black silk jersey, V-neck, underdress in black silk crepe with crew neck, pleated front with braided motif at the waist. Long sleeves with gathered shoulders. Hook-and-eye fastenings at the centre front.
FAA.GRE.0035

no. 29
Repr. p. 95
Madame Grès
Evening gown
Haute couture, c. 1935–36
Black silk velvet, straight cut with cutout at waist. Broad straps, draped panel attached at collarbone level at the front and draped over the right shoulder. Adjustable hook-and-eye fastenings inside the waistband.
FAA.ALI.0002

no. 30
Madame Grès
Evening gown
Haute couture, c. 1963
Black jersey, asymmetric sheath dress, twisted pleated strap on the left attached to the lower armhole at the back, deep V-back with draped panel, no fastenings, box pleat in rear seam.
FAA.GRE.0405

no. 31
Repr. p. 93
Madame Grès
Day dress
Haute couture, spring–summer 1943
Black silk jersey with pleated front. Mid-length skirt, hook-and-eye fastenings at the centre front, long sleeves with pleated shoulders, symmetrical quilted motif below the waist at the front. Silk crepe lining.
FAA.GRE.0014

no. 32
Repr. p. 91
Madame Grès
Evening gown
Imperial red silk jersey, plunging V-neck, gathered panel attached to the waist on the left, draped over the shoulders and falling down the right side of the body. Peplum-style bodice, fully pleated back. Fastened at the centre front with press studs.
FAA.GRE.0031

no. 33
Madeleine Vionnet
Evening gown
Haute couture, 1924
Black silk crepe, embroidered with gold glass beads in Greek-inspired frieze motif on bodice sides and waist. Square neck with straps and straight skirt.
FAA.VIO.0005

no. 34
Repr. p. 117
Madeleine Vionnet
Evening gown, design no. 4113
Haute couture, spring–summer 1925
Black silk crepe with embroidery by Lesage in silver thread and copper-coloured beads, filling a teardrop-shaped panel on the front and almond-shaped panels on the hips, handkerchief hem.
FAA.VIO.0006

no. 35
Repr. p. 5
Madeleine Vionnet
'Little Horses' evening gown
Haute couture, autumn–winter 1921–22
Cream silk crepe with embroidery by Lesage in a frieze motif, incorporating tube beads, silver glass beads and seed stitch in gold thread. Scoop neck and straight-cut skirt edged with long fringe.
FAA.VIO.0004

no. 36
Repr. p. 111
Madeleine Vionnet
Evening gown and cape, previously owned by Agnes Ernst Meyer, mother of Katharine Graham, publisher of the Washington Post
Haute couture, spring–summer 1937
Dark blue and blood red silk crepe. Sleeveless gown with deep armholes and stand-up collar. A-line silhouette. Cape with reversible hood.
FAA.VIO.0001

no. 37
Repr. pp. 114 and 119
Madeleine Vionnet
Evening gown, design 4558
Haute couture, autumn–winter 1938–39
Black silk velvet with flower-motif panels in fuchsia, pale pink and lavender silk velvet. V-necked bodice, flared skirt, halter neck, low-cut back.
FAA.VIO.0008

no. 38
Repr. p. 114
Madeleine Vionnet
Evening gown, design 4271
Haute couture, spring–summer 1937
Bands of anthracite grey silk organza and black silk mesh. Boat neck, cap sleeves, fitted waist, flared skirt. Slip in anthracite grey organza and blue silk crepe.
FAA.VIO.0007.1-2

no. 39
Madeleine Vionnet
Evening gown
Haute couture, spring–summer 1939
Apricot-coloured silk crepe with decorative elements in bronze. Draped neckline with gold leather halter fastening at back, low-cut back. Fitted waist with two darts, skirt with train.
FAA.VIO.0002

no. 40
Repr. p. 115
Madeleine Vionnet
Evening gown
Haute couture, c. 1933
Indigo silk satin. Boat neck, draped and pleated at shoulders, decorative gathers at waist. Fastened at the back with fabric-covered buttons, rear train.
FAA.VIO.0011

no. 41
Madeleine Vionnet
Evening gown
Haute couture, spring–summer 1922
Cream silk crepe, embroidered frieze of white and silver beads around the bust and hem. Boat neck, deep armholes, long straight-cut skirt.
FAA.VIO.0012

no. 42
Repr. p. 116
Madeleine Vionnet
Day dress
Haute couture, winter 1925
Cream silk crepe, with nature-inspired appliqué motifs in black and cream satin. Pussycat bow and sleeves with ribbon ties.
FAA.VIO.0010

no. 43
Repr. p. 101
Elsa Schiaparelli
Evening gown
Haute couture, spring–summer 1939
Ivory silk satin with print motif by Marcel Vertès, depicting elegant ladies walking their dogs, wearing late 19th-century gowns in shades of yellow, blue and lavender. Scoop neckline with four pleats, thin straps overlaid with origami-style folded fabric motifs, which extend to frame the plunge back. Fitted waist, straight skirt, bustle and gathers falling to the rear hem.
FAA.SCH.0018

no. 44
Repr. p. 98
Elsa Schiaparelli
Evening gown
Haute couture, autumn–winter 1934–35
Black silk crepe and tulle with a cascade of rhodoid acetate sequins. V-neck sheath with apron-effect front and plunge back.
FAA.SCH.0054

no. 45
Elsa Schiaparelli
Evening gown
Haute couture, autumn–winter 1936–37
Deep purple waxed silk satin with gold leather border around hem of overskirt, painted and embroidered in metallic thread. Shoulder straps with draped panel around the shoulders, long straight underskirt.
FAA.SCH.0054

no. 46
Repr. p. 97
Elsa Schiaparelli
'Zodiac' jacket from the 'Astrology' collection, possibly worn by Marlene Dietrich in 1938
Haute couture, autumn–winter 1938–39
Navy blue silk velvet, with embroidery by Lesage featuring twelve gold Zodiac symbols along the jacket's edges, framed with diamante and bands of crushed metallic fabric. The front and back panels are adorned with stardust made from glass tube beads, embroidered constellations in diamante and gold thread, shooting stars made of glass and embroidered comets. Shallow V-neckline with slightly raised collar at the back.
FAA.SCH.0001

no. 47
Elsa Schiaparelli
Jacket
Haute couture, c. 1937–39
Black wool crepe, small shawl collar and storm-flaps on the bodice, single-breasted with buttons designed by Jean Clément, made from black lacquered porcelain in the shape of pine cones.
FAA.SCH.0044

no. 48
Elsa Schiaparelli
Suit
Haute couture, 1938
Ensemble comprising a jacket and skirt in wool crepe. Turn-back double collar, peplum at hip level, two sewn-in pockets. Fastened at the centre front with two buttons designed by jeweller Jean Clément, made of gilded metal, resin and paper with engraved decoration and red watercolour paint.
FAA.SCH.0008.1-2

no. 49
Elsa Schiaparelli
Dress, design no. 424
Haute couture, c. 1940
Black silk crepe with embroidery by Lesage, appliqué yoke in pink satin embroidered with arabesque motif in metallic bronze thread and metallic sequins. Small stand-up collar, puff sleeves gathered at the wrist with tasselled bronze ties, dropped V-waist, flowing skirt with frill.
FAA.SCH.0086

no. 50
Repr. p. 105
Paul Poiret
'Tanger' ensemble, from the personal wardrobe of Denise Boulet Poiret
Haute couture, c. 1919–20
Coat and dress in heavy brown wool. Embroidered geometric motifs in coloured cotton with silk tassels. Flared dress, boat neck with white silk trim, seams highlighted with coloured embroidery, half-length raglan sleeves, frilled lace cuffs. Burnous-style cape with full hood, gathered yokes at the front and back, hand slits in the side seams.
FAA.POI.0001.1-2

no. 51
Paul Poiret
Evening gown
Haute couture, c. 1925
Bronze lamé silk serge, embroidered with metallic thread and bronze beads. Pearl straps, draped skirt gathered into a flounce on the left hip, trimmed with embroidered and beaded medallion.
FAA.POI.0003

no. 52
Paul Poiret
Dress
Haute couture, c. 1915–25
Blue silk velvet with embroidered motif in beige and lamé thread. Square neckline edged with pink silk satin and embroidery in metallic thread.
FAA.POI.0006

no. 53
Repr. p. 107
Paul Poiret
'Moscovite' jacket, from the personal wardrobe of Denise Boulet Poiret
Haute couture, c. 1912
Green duvetyne edged with a silk braid printed with the same floral motif as the lining, based on a design by the Atelier Martine. Wrapover front in the style of Russian coachmen's coats, raglan sleeves, black and gold braid. Asymmetric fastening with passementerie buttons.
FAA.POI.0007

no. 54
Paul Poiret
Dress
Haute couture, *c.* 1920–25
Black silk velvet, embroidered medallion with beads and diamante, gathers decorated with scattered cabochons and beads. Deep V-neckline with beaded edging and green satin yoke, short raised collar at the back, silver lamé cuffs.
FAA.POI.0005

no. 55
Repr. pp. 102 and 103
Paul Poiret
Travelling coat, from the personal wardrobe of Denise Boulet Poiret
Haute couture, *c.* 1920
Cream wool with brown stripes woven by Rodier, inspired by North Africa. High stand-up collar with asymmetric buttons, cuffed sleeves, drop waist, hidden pockets. Pongee silk lining printed with a lozenge motif in shades of grey and stylized leaves in peacock blue by Raoul Dufy.
FAA.POI.0002

no. 56
Repr. p. 104
Paul Poiret
Evening gown
Haute couture, *c.* 1920s
Black and ivory silk taffeta, black silk organza, appliqué of guipure lace and beaded braid with silk fringed edging. Scoop neckline, underdress in cream silk crepe and cotton serge.
FAA.POI.0004

no. 57
Repr. p. 87
Chanel
Evening gown
Haute couture, 1937
Brown silk tulle decorated with bands of puckered bronze fabric. Square neckline, bronze grosgrain straps covered in brown tulle, draped shawl panel at the back. Fitted bodice, flared skirt with two box pleats at the back, brown tulle petticoat. Shot silk faille lining.
FAA.CHA.0001

no. 58
Repr. p. 85
Chanel
Evening gown
Haute couture, 1930
Apricot silk organdie with petal-motif appliqué decoration in the same fabric. Shoulder straps, loose bodice, flared skirt.
FAA.CHA.0002

no. 59
Repr. p. 89
Chanel
Evening gown
Haute couture, *c.* 1930
Black silk satin, crossover bodice, wide back, capelet with rounded shoulders and pointed ends. Circular panelled skirt.
FAA.CHA.0003

no. 60
Repr. p. 42
Charles James
Coat
Haute couture, *c.* 1953
Brushed wool serge in ecru, rounded lapels, fitted waist, false peplum, two large diagonal pockets with rounded flaps. Fastened at the centre front with large fabric-covered buttons.
FAA.CHJ.0003

no. 61
Repr. p. 109
Bruyère
Coat
Haute couture, *c.* 1948
Moss green corduroy velvet, rounded collar. Fastened with two ceramic buttons at the centre front. Two oversized patch pockets.
FAA.BRU.0001

no. 62
Repr. p. 63
Busvine
Riding habit
1910s
Jacket, skirt and belt in charcoal grey wool. Double-breasted tailored jacket with fitted waist, lapel collar, two pockets with flaps, fastened at the centre front with two buttons made of black acetate and one made of mother-of-pearl, sleeves with notched cuffs, vent at the centre back, belt, apron-style skirt.
FAA.BUS.0001.1-2

no. 63
Repr. p. 109
Jacques Griffe
Coat
Haute couture, 1949
Apricot-coloured needlecord velvet. Collar with pointed tips, puffed sleeves, organ pleats on the shoulders to create volume. Front fastening with 22 gold buttons
FAA.GRI.0001

no. 64
Repr. p. 60
Doucet
Evening cape
Haute couture, *c.* 1885
Moss green plush velvet, collar and hem embellished with ready-made embroidered braid featuring metallic, faceted and bronze beads. Beaded fringe, silk satin lining, hook-and-eye fastenings.
FAA.DOU.0002

no. 65
Repr. p. 61
Jacques Doucet
Day ensemble
Haute couture, *c.* 1900–05
Jacket and skirt. Figured silk satin, sky blue silk faille, woven hydrangea motif in silk thread. Stand-up collar, lapels and belt in moss green silk velvet. Chantilly or Goncharova-style machine-made lace on the cuffs and yoke, edging a pleated panel of ivory chiffon. Puff sleeves, skirt with train.
FAA.DOU.0001.1-3

no. 66
Repr. p. 53
Charles Frederick Worth
Visite coat
Haute couture, *c.* 1890
Ciselé silk velvet on a base of raspberry pink satin, silk tone-on-tone braiding and twisted metallic gold cord. Raspberry pink chenille fringing on the stand-up collar, front edges, hem and cuffs. Cream silk plush lining.
FAA.WOR.0004

no. 67
Repr. p. 53
Charles Frederick Worth
Evening cape
Haute couture, *c.* 1890
Red silk velvet with appliqué border of vintage needle lace (reticella or cutwork) around the neckline. Collar of frilled black chiffon.
FAA.WOR.0002

no. 68
Repr. pp. 54–55 (detail)
Charles Frederick Worth
Coat
Haute couture, *c.* 1890
Beige wool serge trimmed with ivory duchesse satin, embroidered in ivory, pistachio green and metallic thread. V-collar, embroidered front panel, leg-of-mutton sleeves with turn-up cuffs.
FAA.WOR.0003

no. 69
Repr. p. 57
Redfern
Bodice and skirt
Haute couture, *c.* 1890–1900
Brick red wool with braid, embroidery and astrakhan decoration. Stand-up collar, boned waist, fastened on the left side with fabric-covered buttons.
FAA.RED.0001.1-3

no. 70
Redfern
Coat
Haute couture, *c.* 1890
Figured velvet on an apricot satin base. Stand-up collar, cuffs and hem trimmed with braid and silk satin grosgrain. Fastened at the centre front with twelve fabric-covered buttons, lining of champagne-coloured silk faille.
FAA.RED.0002

no. 71
Repr. p. 59
Anonymous
Visite coat
c. 1875–80
Multicoloured cashmere in shades including red, plum, blue and golden yellow. Flat lapels with plum-coloured grosgrain tie, cuffs and hem trimmed with silk fringing in matching shades, decorative bow on rear. Lining of plum-coloured shot taffeta.
FAA.ANO.0005

no. 72
Anonymous
Bolero
c. 1900
Purple silk velvet with appliquéd bands of braided ribbon, jet and glass beads. Stand-up collar, stripe motif on the collar, hem and cuffs, beaded fringe on hem.
FAA.ANO.0001

no. 73
Repr. pp. 123 and 124–125
Boué Soeurs
'Lamballe' dress
Haute couture, 1923–25
Metallic lace mesh, appliqué in silk lamé with embroidery, beads and ribbons. Scoop neck with straps, wide belt in metallic fabric with stem stitch and cannetille tassels, panniers on the hips, beaded fringing on the hem.
FAA.BOU.0001

no. 74
Repr. p. 129
Lenief
Dress
Haute couture, *c.* 1920
Olive green silk velvet with metallic sequins and gold lamé. Sweetheart neckline, scalloped front panel with appliqué design in gold lamé. Welt pockets with embroidered trim, flared sleeves and mid-length skirt in pleated gold lamé.
FAA.LEN.0001

no. 75
Repr. p. 20
Jenny
Travelling coat
Gold wool with woven pointillist-style dot motif and woven stripes on the cuffs and pockets. Small lapel collar, button fastening, hip-length capelet.
FAA.JEN.0003

no. 76
Jenny
Evening gown
Haute couture, *c.* 1930
Apricot silk satin. Deep V-neckline, bodice gathered into front panel, fitted skirt with diamond-shaped panels. Matching capelet in the same fabric.
FAA.JEN.0002.1-2

no. 77
Jenny
Afternoon dress
Haute couture, *c.* 1922
Russet chiffon, boat neck, long sleeves, bands of decorative beading in shades of russet.
FAA.JEN.0001.1-2

no. 78
Paquin
Evening coat
Haute couture, *c.* 1925
Base layer of undyed cotton, Cornely embroidery in metallic gold thread, orange silk thread, plant motifs in metallic silver thread, green and grey silk thread, appliqué motifs in multicoloured silk velvet. Small stand-up collar, straight sleeves, flared shape, figured satin lining.
FAA.PAQ.0001

no. 79
Repr. p. 138
Paquin
Evening gown
Haute couture, autumn–winter 1937–38
Black silk jersey, cords of braided gold laminette around the cuffs and in a vertical band down the centre front, on a ground of gathered black chiffon. V-neck with lapel collar, full-length pencil skirt.
FAA.PAQ.0002

no. 80
Repr. p. 141
Jean Patou
Dress
Haute couture, *c.* 1930
Dark blue satin, sleeveless with asymmetric neckline, matching belt.
FAA.PAT.0003

no. 81
Jean Patou
Evening gown
Haute couture, *c.* 1930
Black silk crepe georgette with panels of self-coloured silk satin, metal Art Deco brooch with rhinestone gem. Square neckline cinched by brooch at centre front, low-cut back. Bow on back of waist, skirt with two-panelled train, pointed hem.
FAA.PAT.0001

no. 82
Repr. p. 143
Jean Patou
Dress and jacket, from the personal wardrobe of Mademoiselle Jack, a model for Patou in the 1930s
Haute couture, c. 1935–38
Light blue silk crepe with darker blue and pink panels. Boat neck front and low-cut back, lightly gathered shoulders, band of pink crepe with cut-out motif around the waist. Short jacket in light and dark blue silk crepe with long sleeves and gathered shoulders.
FAA.PAT.0004.1-2

no. 83
Jean Patou
Dress
Haute couture, 1930s
Ivory silk crepe with floral print. Asymmetric neckline, low-cut draped back, tie belt.
FAA.PAT.0006

no. 84
Repr. p. 142
Jean Patou
Dress and bolero
Haute couture, c. 1939
Black silk crepe, bands of black glass beading around the waist. Long sheath dress with boat neck. Bolero embroidered all over with black tube beads, on a ground of black crepe georgette.
FAA.PAT.0002.1-2

no. 85
Jean Patou
Day ensemble
Haute couture, c. 1924–29
Dress and coat. Coat made of black wool serge, lapel collar, flower in the same printed fabric as the dress and lining, welt pockets with flaps, lining of printed silk crepe. Dress in silk crepe with floral print.
FAA.PAT.0005.1-2

no. 86
Nina Ricci
Dress and bolero
Haute couture, c. 1937
Silk crepe in diagonal bands of royal blue and fuchsia pink, ostrich feather flounces on the bodice, sleeves and hem.
FAA.RIC.0001.1-2

no. 87
Repr. pp. 126 and 127
Lenief
Cape
Haute couture, c. 1925–30
Cardinal red silk velvet, gold lamé lining. Cut-out plunging back with tassel of braided gold thread. Broad velvet panels in the same shade of red draped from the shoulders.
FAA.LEN.0002

no. 88
Repr. pp. 130 and 131
Mariano Fortuny
Cape
Haute couture, c. 1925–30
Brown panne velvet with gold all-over stripe print and stylized floral panels. Keyhole neckline, pointed hood with two toggles and gold braid fastenings, collar fastened with six large beads of varnished wood.
FAA.FOR.0001

no. 89
Mariano Fortuny
Evening coat
Haute couture, c 1925–30
Fur trimmed with Murano beads, woodblock-printed with plant motif. Broad shawl collar, straight sleeves.
FAA.FOR.0002

no. 90
Repr. pp. 132 and 133
Myrbor
Coat
Haute couture, c. 1925–30
Brown silk velvet with panels of geometric embroidery in gold and silver metallic thread.
FAA.MYR.0001

no. 91
Repr. pp. 134 and 135
Callot Soeurs
Coat
Haute couture, c. 1920s
Pongee (wool and silk) jacquard with woven plant motifs in metallic thread, collar and trim in blue-purple silk satin.
FAA.CAL.0001

no. 92
Repr. p. 149
Manguin
Dress
Haute couture, c. 1948–50
Bodice and skirt, base layer of coral taffeta overlaid with purple-brown chiffon. Bodice fastened at the centre back with fabric-covered buttons. Buttons on the sleeve cuffs. Asymmetric draped skirt with train attached to belt, bubble hem.
FAA.MAN.0001.1-2

no. 93
Philippe & Gaston
Dress
Haute couture, c. 1930
Cream serge, metallic and cream silk thread. Diagonal bodice with triangular cut-outs, cream silk organza lining.
FAA.PHI.0001

no. 94
Repr. p. 147
Raphaël
Evening gown
Haute couture, c. 1947–50
Cream silk jersey, spaghetti straps, draped fabric over smocked bodice.
FAA.RAP.0002

no. 95
Mainbocher
Evening gown
Haute couture, c. 1930
Ivory silk satin, square neckline with ribbon straps, fabric-covered spherical buttons, full-length skirt.
FAA.MAI.0001

no. 96
Repr. p. 137
Augustabernard
Evening gown
Haute couture, autumn–winter 1933–34
Cream silk crepe with mauve-grey panels creating a *trompe-l'oeil* bolero effect. Boat neck and mauve-grey panel around waist.
FAA.AUG.0001

no. 97
Repr. p. 145
Molyneux
Day dress
Haute couture, c. 1938–40
Dark purple-brown silk jersey, V-neck and gathered front, flowing skirt and deep patch pockets. Brown silk crepe lining.
FAA.MOL.0001

no. 98
Repr. p. 154
Jeanne Lanvin
'Sarah' dress
Mid-season 1936
Navy blue silk crepe, hand-sewn with metallic silver studs and silver sequins. Draped scoop front and keyhole back with loose ribbon straps. No label.
FAA.LAN.0001.1-2

no. 99
Jeanne Lanvin
Evening gown, design no. 21652
Haute couture, c. 1935
Moroccan crepe in celadon blue, square sailor collar, quilted and embroidered with concentric rows of metallic gold thread, low-cut back. Belt in the same fabric, gold butterfly-shaped buckle.
FAA.LAN.0002.1-2

no. 100
Repr. p. 156
Jeanne Lanvin
'Matho' evening cape
Haute couture, autumn–winter 1935–36
Crimson wool crepe and duchesse satin decorated with bands of satin stitch. Broad collar with large conical button.
FAA.LAN.0004

no. 101
Repr. p. 153
Jeanne Lanvin
'Bouclier' evening gown
Haute couture, 1934
Black silk crepe with three large gold appliqué medallions on the chest and back. High slash neck, kimono-style sleeve openings.
FAA.LAN.0007

no. 102
Jeanne Lanvin
Coat
Haute couture, spring–summer 1939
Front panels and cuffs of glazed satin, quilted and embroidered, full skirt with godets. Revere collar, centre front fastened with large square lacquered and faceted buttons.
FAA.LAN.0005

no. 103
Repr. p. 151
Jeanne Lanvin
'Lohengrin' evening coat
Haute couture, spring–summer 1931
Copper-coloured lamé embroidered with chain stitch in opal green. Broad shawl collar, full curved sleeves with central pleat and stitched stripes radiating from inside the elbow. Apple green silk satin lining with the same embroidered motif visible on the inside.
FAA.LAN.0003

no. 104
Repr. p. 158
Lucien Lelong
Evening gown
Haute couture, c. 1938
Black silk jersey with panels of self-coloured silk lace. Sheath dress with V-neckline and straps, fitted and draped waist, full-length skirt with lace panel.
FAA.LEL.0001

no. 105
Repr. p. 161
Lucien Lelong
Evening gown
Haute couture, c. 1925–30
Chocolate brown silk velvet, diamante shoulder decorations and tulip sleeves. V-neckline, draped bodice, buckled belt in the same fabric with diamante decoration.
FAA.LEL.0002.1-2

no. 106
Lucien Lelong
Evening gown
Haute couture, c. 1945–50
Deep blue silk crepe, asymmetric draped armholes, draped bodice, full-length skirt.
FAA.LEL.0003

no. 107
Robert Piguet
Cocktail dress
Haute couture, c. 1938–40
Bias-cut wool crepe in fuchsia pink. V-neckline, draped wrapover bodice, long sleeves, skirt made up of diagonal panels with V-shaped pleats, satin lining.
FAA.PIG.0001

no. 108
Repr. p. 163
Robert Piguet
Cocktail dress
Haute couture, c. 1940
Black velvet bustier bodice with halter strap, low-cut back and boned waist. Luneville embroidery with tube beads and sequins, appliqué design in velvet around the top of the skirt.
FAA.PIG.0002

no. 109
Jacques Griffe
Coat
Haute couture, c. 1948–50
Black silk taffeta, lapel collar, two large angled patch pockets with wide flaps. Centre front fastening with black acetate buttons. Silk satin lining.
FAA.GRI.0003

no. 110
Repr. p. 165
Jacques Griffe
Evening ensemble
Haute couture, c. 1948–50
Black tulle bustier dress. Draped bodice cut low at the back, full skirt decorated with appliqué stripes in white, cream and pearl pink tulle forming a border and bow motif at the hem.
FAA.GRI.0002.1-2

no. 111
Balmain
House dress
Haute couture, c. 1948–50
Dusky pink wool serge, V-neckline with self-coloured buttons to the hem. Dolman sleeves, self-coloured belt, skirt with bands of dusky pink fringing.
FAA.BAM.0001.1-2

no. 112
Repr. p. 169
Jean Dessès
Evening gown, which possibly belonged to Margot Fonteyn, the British ballerina who formed a celebrated dance partnership with Rudolf Nureyev
Haute couture, c. 1960
Black chiffon and duchesse satin. Bustier bodice with low-cut back, draped rear panel, bubble hem.
FAA.DES.0004

no. 113
Jean Dessès
Dress
Haute couture, c. 1950
Black silk velvet, V-neckline with
asymmetric buttons, long sleeves,
cape-effect shoulders, waist with
vertical seams, draped fabric panel,
full skirt with asymmetric train.
FAA.DES.0002

no. 114
Repr. p. 167
Jean Dessès
Cocktail dress
Haute couture, c. 1958
Black organza, crossover neckline, low-cut
V-shaped back, waist accentuated by a
belt, full skirt with layered fabric petals
over a horsehair stiffened petticoat,
boned bodice.
FAA.DES.0003

no. 115
Repr. p. 179
Christian Dior
'Maréchal' dress
Haute couture, autumn–winter 1958–59
Black silk velvet with sash in pale pink
duchesse satin.
FAA.DIO.0004

no. 116
Repr. p. 182
Christian Dior
Cocktail ensemble
Haute couture, c. 1950
Dress and bolero made of black silk
taffeta and silk tulle. Bolero with
exaggerated shawl collar, tied with
front bow. Black pongee silk lining.
FAA.DIO.0008

no. 117
Repr. p. 177
Christian Dior by Yves Saint Laurent
Cocktail dress, 'Trapeze' line
Haute couture, spring–summer 1958
Black 'Alaskine' (a wool and silk serge,
believed to have been invented by the
Lyon-based silk manufacturer Staron to
mark the 49th star – representing the state
of Alaska – being added to the flag of the
United States in 1959). Flared trapeze-line
cut, high waistline with appliqué bow at
the centre front, fastened at the centre
back with seven black acetate buttons.
FAA.DIO.0005

no. 118
Christian Dior
'Astarté' cocktail dress,
Haute couture, spring–summer 1955
Black silk taffeta, integrated bodice,
shoulder bows, skirt with box pleats.
FAA.DIO.0007

no. 119
Repr. p. 174
Jacques Fath
Day dress
Haute couture, c. 1952–54
Black duchesse satin with short
V-collar, long sleeves, straight-cut
skirt with asymmetric draped panel,
button fastening.
FAA.FAT.0005

no. 120
Repr. p. 173
Jacques Fath
Evening gown
Haute couture, c. 1949–50
Black silk velvet and taffeta. Stand-up
collar, buttons at the centre front,
full-length skirt, draped train and bow
at back in charcoal grey silk.
FAA.FAT.0003

no. 121
Jacques Fath
Dress
Haute couture, c. 1948
Silk taffeta, silk tulle and figured silk edged
with bands of black guipure lace. Deep
V-neckline, half-length sleeves, full-length
skirt with front pleated panel.
FAA.FAT.0001

no. 122
Repr. p. 171
Jacques Fath
*Ballgown, formerly belonging to
Enid Lindeman, Countess of Kenmare
(Australia), who lived in Saint-Jean-
Cap-Ferrat, France*
Haute couture, c. 1940
Brown silk velvet bodice embroidered with
gold sequins, glass beads and gold tassels.
Waist accentuated by an embroidered
band, skirt made up of silk velvet panels
in autumnal shades of brown, grey,
russet and moss green.
FAA.FAT.0002

no. 123
Repr. p. 174
Jacques Fath
Day dress
Haute couture, c. 1952–54
Black wool crepe and shot silk taffeta.
V-neckline, five black buttons, long
sleeves. Straight-cut skirt with
symmetrical draped effect
FAA.FAT.0004

no. 124
Hubert de Givenchy
'Colette' evening gown, design no. 19
Haute couture, 1959
Black lace and horsehair embroidered all
over with organza strips, two black satin
bows on the waist and left shoulder.
FAA.GIV.0001

no. 125
Rudi Gernreich
Dress
Ready-to-wear, c. 1972
Bodice with black ribbed wool jersey
front and transparent chiffon back.
Short sleeves, long skirt gathered at the
waist with pockets in the side seams.
Zip fastening at the centre front.
FAA.GER.0001

no. 126
André Courrèges
Evening gown, worn by Marisa Berenson
Haute couture, 1968
Trapeze cut, round neck, sleeveless.
Embroidered with geometric motifs in
black sequins on a background of black
tulle, pale-coloured lining.
FAA.COU.0001

no. 127
Repr. p. 189
Pierre Cardin
Dress
Haute couture, 1969
Trapeze cut in black wool crepe, round
neckline, sleeveless, with pleats falling
from the bust to the bubble hem.
FAA.CAR.0001.1-2

no. 128
Repr. p. 185
Yves Saint Laurent
Evening gown
Haute couture, autumn–winter 1962–63
Black silk crepe, integrated bustier in
black silk tulle, long straight-cut skirt
with draped detail and bow at knee level.
FAA.YSL.0003

no. 129
Repr. p. 187
Yves Saint Laurent
*Evening gown, design no. 74, worn
by Danielle Luquet de Saint Germain*
Haute couture, autumn–winter 1968–69
Black chiffon, round neck, embellished
with a band of ostrich feathers around
the hips.
FAA.YSL.0004

no. 130
Repr. p. 193
Alexander McQueen
Evening gown, look 43
Ready-to-wear, autumn–winter 2007–08
Black hammered satin crepe, V-neckline
and train. Embellished with silver glass
tube beads forming a motif of tumbling
tresses of hair falling from the neckline.
FAA.MCQ.0001

no. 131
Repr. p. 197
Thierry Mugler
Evening gown
Ready-to-wear, autumn–winter 1987–88
Black panne velvet, draped plunge back
edged with broad pearl pink satin collar.
FAA.MUG.0001

no. 132
Repr. p. 205
Comme des Garçons
Dress, look 12
Ready-to-wear, spring–summer 2014
Tulle, jersey, viscose, bows and fringing
in shades of black. Pyramid-shaped
framework, high collar, sleeveless.
FAA.CDG.0001

no. 133
Repr. pp. 201 and 202–203
Junya Watanabe
Dress, look 19
Ready-to-wear, spring–summer 2005
V-neckline bodice made from multiple
bronze zip fastenings. Low-cut back
and flared skirt in black cotton with
raw-edge hem.
FAA.JUN.0001

no. 134
Repr. p. 33
Yohji Yamamoto
Dress
Ready-to-wear, summer 2008
Black chiffon. Double straps, simple
straight cut, gathered fabric panels
cascading down from top of bodice.
FAA.YAM.0002

no. 135
Repr. p. 195
Christian Dior by John Galliano
Evening gown, look 46
Ready-to-wear, spring–summer 2000
Pale blue-green satin with woven floral
medallion motifs. Unstructured shape with
zips and cut-outs, pockets and panels,
puff sleeves, asymmetric hem and train.
FAA.GAL.0001

no. 136
Repr. p. 199
Jean Paul Gaultier
Trenchcoat dress, look 19
Haute couture, autumn–winter 2010–11
Black acetate and rayon crepe. Double-
breasted effect, lapel collar, storm flaps on
chest and back, epaulettes and adjustable
cuffs. Buckled belt made of the same
fabric, miniskirt front and full-length back.
FAA.JPG.0001

no. 137
Balenciaga by Nicolas Ghesquière
Dress, look 36
Ready-to-wear, autumn–winter 2004–05
Black chiffon and printed jersey with black
metallic chain trim. Asymmetric cut-outs,
V-neckline and draped panel skirt.
FAA.GHE.0001

no. 138
Vivienne Westwood
Ensemble
Ready-to-wear, c. 2000
Skirt and corset in gold satin, striped
red and cream jersey and cream
cotton. Boned bodice with off-the-
shoulder neckline, balloon sleeves and
yoke with braid made of grey cotton
jersey, zip fastening at the centre front.
Pencil skirt with flared hem, belt made
of striped jersey.
FAA.VIV.0001.1-2

no. 139
Repr. p. 211
Henri Matisse, for *The Song of the
Nightingale*, an adaptation of Igor
Stravinsky's opera commissioned by
Sergei Diaghilev for the Ballets Russes
Stage costume: 'Mandarin'
First performance on 2 February 1920
at the Opéra de Paris
Golden yellow shot silk satin, trapeze
line, stand-up collar fastened with three
buttons, long kimono sleeves, flower
motifs with petals hand-painted in black
ink and padded centres covered in yellow
and metallic gold thread, whole garment
quilted, with cheesecloth lining.
FAA.BAR.0001

no. 140
Repr. p. 209
Henri Matisse, for *The Song of the
Nightingale*, an adaptation of Igor
Stravinsky's opera commissioned by
Sergei Diaghilev for the Ballets Russes
Stage costume: 'Mourner'
First performance on 2 February 1920
at the Opéra de Paris
Dress and hood made of light beige wool
felt. Hood with long rectangular panel
falling from the back, with appliqué
chevron motif in dark blue velvet.
Bow-style motif on the forehead and two
stiff stand-up 'ears'. Trapeze-line dress,
round collar, all-over appliqué motif
of dark blue velvet triangles.
FAA.BAR.0002.1-2

no. 141
Henri Matisse, for *The Song of the
Nightingale*, adaptation of Igor
Stravinsky's opera commissioned by
Sergei Diaghilev for the Ballets Russes
Stage costume: 'Mourner'
First performance on 2 February 1920
at the Opéra de Paris
Dress and hood made of light beige wool
felt. Hood with long rectangular panel
falling from the back, with appliqué
chevron motif in dark blue velvet.
Bow-style motif on the forehead and two
stiff stand-up 'ears'. Trapeze-line dress,
round collar, all-over appliqué motif
of dark blue velvet triangles.
FAA.BAR.0003.1-2

AZZEDINE ALAÏA:
A BRIEF BIOGRAPHY

1935

Azzedine Ben Alaya is born on 26 February in Tunis, Tunisia.

1950

Madame Pineau, the French midwife who was present at his birth, introduces him to the world of art and fashion, and enrols him at the Tunis Institute of Fine Arts.

The young Azzedine learns to sew with his sister Hafida and funds his studies by working for dressmakers such as Madame Richard, who buys haute couture patterns in Paris and recreates them.

1956

He arrives in Paris and starts an internship at Christian Dior, but leaves after four days. Simone Zehrfuss, the wife of architect Bernard Zehrfuss, introduces him to Parisian high society, where he meets César, Joan Miró, Charlotte Perriand and Louise de Vilmorin.

1958–1959

Alaïa starts working for couturier Guy Laroche, where his friend Leila Menchari is an in-house model. He works there for three seasons.

Countess Nicole de Blégiers welcomes him into her home.

He starts dressing private clients, including high society women such as Cécile, Lina and Marie-Hélène de Rothschild.

1960

Alaïa meets Arletty and starts designing clothes for her. The iconic actress's style and films inspire many of his collections.

1963

He meets Lison Bonfils, a model for Christian Dior, and Bettina Graziani, a model for Jacques Fath.

1964

He moves to 60 rue de Bellechasse (7th *arrondissement*) on the left bank, where he sets up his fashion house. He designs clothes for private clients at the same time as working on commissions for other fashion houses.

He buys his first major work of art, a Coptic sculpture of a head that is believed to have belonged to Countess Greffulhe.

He changes the spelling of his surname to 'Alaïa'.

1967–1969

When the House of Balenciaga closes, Alaïa buys some of the great Spanish couturier's gowns. This is the spark that begins the building of a collection of pieces by iconic fashion designers.

1971

He meets Greta Garbo, who commissions a number of pieces from him, including coats in a masculine style.

He works on a number of collections for the designer Christiane Bailly.

1979

The fashion designer Thierry Mugler asks Alaïa to make some suits and encourages him to design his own collections.

Alaïa designs a ready-to-wear collection for Charles Jourdan, featuring leather garments adorned with metal studs, but it is rejected as too daring.

1981

Lison Bonfils introduces him to Silvia Bocchese, president of the Italian knitwear manufacturer Maglificio Miles. It is the start of a collaboration and a friendship that will last a lifetime.

1982

In September, after seeing Bill Cunningham's photographs of Alaïa's work in *WWD* (*Women's Wear Daily*), Dawn Mello invites Alaïa to hold a runway show in the New York department store Bergdorf Goodman.

1983

He launches his label 'Alaïa' and presents his first spring–summer runway show at the rue de Bellechasse.

1984

Alaïa moves to a private mansion at 17 rue du Parc-Royal (3rd *arrondissement*), decorated by Andrée Putnam.

1985

He presents his designs from the previous three years at the Palladium in New York. The set is designed by Jean-Paul Goude and the show features more than fifty models. It is attended by over a thousand guests, including Andy Warhol, all of whom are asked to dress in black.

The French Ministry of Culture honours the couturier's work at its annual fashion awards, awarding him two prizes: 'Best French Collection' and 'Designer of the Year'.

The exhibition 'A Day with Azzedine Alaïa: Fashion, 1980–1985' is held at CAPC, a contemporary art museum in Bordeaux, curated by Jean-Louis Froment.

Alaïa designs Grace Jones's costumes for the James Bond film *A View to a Kill*, directed by John Glen.

1986

Naomi Campbell makes her runway debut in Azzedine Alaïa's show.

The couturier becomes friends with Tina Turner and designs stage costumes for her.

1987

Alaïa buys a group of 19th-century buildings at 18 rue de la Verrerie, in Paris's 4th *arrondissement*. He renovates them and moves his apartment, his studio and his boutique there. He starts holding runway shows in the grand glass-ceilinged hall.

1988

The first Alaïa boutique opens in New York, featuring furniture by Julian Schnabel.

The spring–summer 1988 collection is presented at Alaïa's premises on the rue de la Verrerie in May, two months after most of the Paris runway shows. From then on, Alaïa decides to hold shows on his own schedule and steps back from the official fashion calendar.

1989

To mark the bicentenary of the French Revolution, French Minister of Culture Jack Lang commissions Jean-Paul Goude to organize a parade on 14 July. Alaïa designs a dress based on the French flag, which is worn by Jessye Norman when she sings the French national anthem in the Place de la Concorde, Paris.

Alaïa becomes a French citizen.

1991

Azzedine begins a collaboration with the popular label Tati, creating a collection inspired by its famous pink gingham.

1992–1999

The spring–summer 1992 collection is accompanied by the first book about the couturier's work, published by Prosper Assouline.

Alaïa retreats from the fashion world for a while after the death of his sister Hafida. Although he is no longer putting on runway shows, he continues to design haute couture clothing for private clients and to sell his ready-to-wear line in some stores. These are years of research and experimentation for the couturier.

In 1996, the Palazzo Corsini in Florence holds the first retrospective of Alaïa's work, curated by Carla Sozzani.

In 1997, an exhibition held at the Groninger Museum, curated by Mark Wilson, displays Alaïa's designs alongside works by Basquiat, César, Pablo Picasso, Julian Schnabel and Andy Warhol.

In 1999, Carla Sozzani helps Alaïa to relaunch his fashion house, with financial support from Giuliano Coppini, founder of the thread manufacturer Lineapiú.

Maryline Vigouroux invites Alaïa to become honorary president of the Mediterranean Fashion Institute.

2000–2002

The Prada Group invests in the Alaïa brand.

In 2000, Alaïa exhibits his designs at the Guggenheim Museum SoHo in New York, alongside Andy Warhol's *Last Supper* paintings.

He holds a runway show for his summer 2002 collection at the boutique at 7 rue de Moussy (4th *arrondissement*).

2003

Alaïa presents his first exclusively haute couture runway show, which revisits his most iconic fashion designs.

2004–2017

He founds the Galerie Azzedine Alaïa at 18 rue de la Verrerie (4th *arrondissement*). He opens the doors of his fashion house, exhibiting work by major and emerging talents in the fields of art, fashion, design, photography and literature until 2017.

2005

Alaïa holds an exhibition of pieces from the personal wardrobe of Denise Poiret at his gallery, ahead of an auction held by Piasa at the Hotel Drouot on 10 and 11 May 2005. He buys a number of Paul Poiret designs at the auction.

2007

Alaïa sells his company to the Richemont Group.

With his partner and Carla Sozzani, he sets up the Association Azzedine Alaïa, to preserve his collection of fashion, design and art.

2009

The Galerie Azzedine Alaïa holds an exhibition of around forty dresses by Elsa Schiaparelli before they are auctioned by Drouot.

2011–2013

The exhibition 'Alaïa: Azzedine Alaïa in the 21st Century' opens at the Groninger Museum in 2011, then moves to the Kunstpalast in Dusseldorf in 2013.

In 2013, Alaïa designs the costumes for Mozart's opera *The Marriage of Figaro*, directed by Christopher Alden and performed at the Los Angeles Philharmonic, with sets designed by Jean Nouvel.

That same year, the Palais Galliera, Musée de la Mode de la Ville de Paris, holds the first retrospective of Alaïa's work in the French capital, while the Musée de l'Art Moderne de Paris displays some of his most iconic designs in its Matisse Room.

2015

The exhibition 'Couture/Sculpture' is held at the Galleria Borghese in Rome.

2017

In July, Alaïa presents his third exclusively haute couture runway show, the winter 2017 collection.

Azzedine Alaïa dies in Paris on 18 November 2017.

The foundation that he wished to create is recognized as an establishment of public utility on 28 February 2020. The Fondation Azzedine Alaïa's mission is to preserve the work of Azzedine Alaïa and the many pieces of art, fashion and design that he collected throughout his life. It holds exhibitions, publishes reference works and supports cultural and educational initiatives.

This catalogue was published on the occasion of the exhibition 'Azzedine Alaïa, couturier collectionneur', presented at the Palais Galliera – Musée de la Mode de la Ville de Paris from 27 September 2023 to 21 January 2024.

Exhibition organized by the Palais Galliera, Musée de la Mode de la Ville de Paris / Paris Musées, in collaboration with the Fondation Azzedine Alaïa and to coincide with the exhibition 'Alaïa / Grès. Au-delà de la mode' at the Fondation Azzedine Alaïa.

Exhibition coordinators:
Miren Arzalluz,
director of the Palais Galliera
Olivier Saillard,
director of the Fondation Azzedine Alaïa with the assistance of Gaël Mamine and Alice Freudiger

Artistic director: Olivier Saillard
Graphics and exhibition design:
Studio Matters
Lighting: ACL

HONORARY COMMITTEE

Anne Hidalgo, *Mayor of Paris*

Carine Rolland, *Deputy Mayor, Head of Culture and the 15-Minute City, president of Paris Musées*

Afaf Gabelotaud, *Deputy Mayor, Head of Business, Employment and Economic Development, vice-president of Paris Musées*

PARIS MUSÉES

Anne-Sophie de Gasquet,
director in chief

PALAIS GALLIERA, MUSÉE DE LA MODE DE PARIS

Miren Arzalluz, *director*
Hugo Lucchino, *general secretary*

Conservation
Laurent Cotta, *collections manager, graphic arts collection*
Pascale Gorguet Ballesteros, *senior curator, 18th-century collections*
Sophie Grossiord, *senior curator, early 20th-century collections to 1947*
Marie-Laure Gutton, *collections manager, accessories*
Marine Kisiel, *curator, 19th-century collections*
Sylvie Lécallier, *collections manager, photographs*
Alexandre Samson, *collections manager, 1947 to present day*
Marie-Ange Bernieri, *administrative manager of collections*
Jacqueline Dumaine and Samy Jelil, *conservation assistants*
Alice Freudiger, *exhibition assistant*

Collections
Véronique Belloir, *head of department*
Isabelle Jolfre, *database administrator*
Emmanuelle Andoren-Lecointre, *digital manager*
Sylvie Brun and Anastasia Ozoline, *textiles restoration*
Camille Lallemand, *paper and leather restoration*

Works management
Hélène Favrel, *head of department*
Corinne Dom, *head of collections management*
Delphine Aubert de Trégomain, Bérénice Collard, Joëlle Duhoo, Thierry Fripier, Chloé Lissonet, Loïcia Margotat, Christine Mebtoul, Georgiana Necualescu, *management assistants*

Library and documents centre
Sylvie Roy, *head of department*
Nathalie Gourseau, *documents manager*

Visitor management
Evren Adanir, *head of department*
Laure Bernard, *visitor coordinator*
Sandra Cominotto, Sylvia Gagin and Charlotte de Percin-Sermet, *guides*
Myriam Loussaief, *visual artist*

Communications
Anne de Nesle, *head of department*
Margaux Brisson, *comms officer*

Administration
Richard Delbourg, *deputy general secretary*
Monique Bouard, Alice Danger and Catherine Gervais, *assistants*
Béatrice Schoeb, *head of commercial development and patrons*

Buildings and security
Prosper Thomas, *head technician*
Jessy Clemendot, *deputy technician*
Élisabeth Thébault, *reception manager*
Jean-Michel Lavenette, *chief officer*
Christophe Marie and Samir Belghit, *safety and security managers*
Dalton Bernard and Alessandro Masini, *chief officers*
And all the reception and security teams

EXHIBITIONS & PUBISHING

Julie Bertrand, *director*

Julie Pierrat, *head of exhibitions department*
Laura Farge, *project manager*
Mathilde Bartier and Alexandra Jouanneau, *production managers*

Éric Landauer, *head of the museum workshops department of the City of Paris,* and his team

Muriel Rausch, *deputy director and head of publishing department*
Nathalie Bec, *editorial project manager*
Amélie Segonds, *picture researcher, assisted by* Iseult Cahen-Patron
Mara Mariano, *head of production*
Marion Assémat, *sales manager*
Claude Ribeiro, *sales administrator*

VISITOR DEVELOPMENT, PARTNERSHIPS & COMMUNICATIONS

Agnès Benayer, *director*
Nina Garnier, *head of comms department*
Blandine Cottet, *deputy head of comms and partnerships*
Florian Brottes, *comms officer*
Andréa Longrais, *press and public relations officer*

Scarlett Greco, *head of digital*
Camille Autran, *digital project manager*

Anne-Claude d'Argent, *head of patrons and commercial activities*
Ludivine Mispelaere, *patron development manager*

Frédérique Leseur, *head of visitors department*
Raffaella Ricci, *media project manager*

ADMINISTRATION & FINANCE

Alice Lebredonchel, *director and deputy general director*

And the whole team at Paris Musées

FONDATION AZZEDINE ALAÏA

President
Carla Sozzani

Director
Olivier Saillard

Archives and conservation
Gaël Mamine
Sarah Perks
Ariel Stark-Ferré
Sandrine Tinturier

Research and documentation
Robinson Boursault
Zoé Guédard

Conservation interns
Gwenn Meunier
Killian Petit
Tayma Debs

General secretary
Bénédicte Breton

ACKNOWLEDGMENTS

Balenciaga
Gaspard de Massé
Archive manager
Léa Blin
Archive assistant

Christian Dior Couture
Olivier Flaviano
Director – Dior La Galerie
Perrine Scherrer
Director of Dior Héritage

Lanvin
Laure Harivel
Heritage & Archives Manager

Musée d'Art Moderne de Paris
Fabrice Hergott
Director

Musée des Arts Décoratifs, Paris
Marie-Sophie Carron de la Carrière
Head curator
Marie Pierre Ribère
Assistant curator
Emmanuelle Blandinières Beauvin
Head of fashion and textiles documentation

Musée Yves Saint Laurent Paris
Serena Bucalo
Curator, collections manager
Domitille Eblé
Head of graphic arts collection

The Museum at FIT, New York
Colleen Hill
Curator of Costumes & Accessories

Schiaparelli
Francesco Pastore
Head of heritage and cultural events
Sonya Parsons
Heritage assistant

Vivienne Westwood Limited
Ellie Boyce
Fashion GPS Co-ordinator & Archivist

Palais Galliera, Musée de la Mode de la Ville de Paris
Véronique Belloir
Head of collections department
Alexandre Samson
Manager of collections from 1947 to contemporary design
Sylvie Roy
Library and documents manager

In memory of
Madame Marie-Andrée Jouve

Éditions Paris Musées

Julie Bertrand
Director
Muriel Rausch
Deputy director, head of publishing

Nathalie Bec
Project editor
Amélie Segonds
assisted by Iseult Cahen-Patron
Picture research
Mara Mariano
Head of production

Publishing secretary
Sylvie Bellu

Art director
Olivier Saillard

Graphic design
Laurent Fétis

Repro
Apex Graphic, Paris

with the collaboration of Alice Freudiger, Gaël Mamine, Ariel Stark-Ferré, Zoé Guédard and Véronique Patard

INDEX OF ILLUSTRATED DESIGNERS

Couturier profiles are by Olivier Saillard.
Those for the Henri Matisse costumes are
by Anastasia Ozoline and Charlotte Barat.

Graphic design and layout: Laurent Fétis

Translated from the French *Azzedine Alaïa.
Couturier collectionneur* by Bethany Wright

First published in the United Kingdom in 2024
by Thames & Hudson Ltd, 181A High Holborn,
London WC1V 7QX

First published in the United States of America in 2024
by Thames & Hudson Inc., 500 Fifth Avenue, New York,
New York 10110

Published in collaboration with the Fondation
Azzedine Alaïa.

Original edition © 2023 Paris Musées, les musées de la
Ville de Paris, for the first edition of the book published in
French on the occasion of the exhibition 'Azzedine Alaïa.
Couturier collectionneur', presented at the Palais Galliera
– Musée de la Mode de la Ville de Paris from 27 September
to 21 January 2024, curated by Miren Arzalluz, Director
of the Palais Galliera and Olivier Saillard, Director of the
Fondation Azzedine Alaïa, assisted by Gaël Mamine and
Alice Freudiger.

This edition © 2024 Thames & Hudson Ltd, London

British Library Cataloguing-in-Publication Data
A catalogue record for this book is available from
the British Library

Library of Congress Control Number 2023948724

ISBN 978-0-500-02813-1

Printed and bound in China by
Toppan Leefung Printing Limited

Be the first to know about our new releases,
exclusive content and author events by visiting
thamesandhudson.com
thamesandhudsonusa.com
thamesandhudson.com.au